THE BOOK FOR MEN WHO HAVE EVERYTHING

Unusual Knowledge and Boredom Busters for Intelligent Men

IQ Street

ISBN: 979-8-89095-060-4
Copyright © 2025 By Curious Press

CONTENTS

INTRODUCTION

Did you know that Corn Flakes were invented when a tray of wheat dough was accidentally left out on a kitchen countertop overnight?

And did you know that a band of Belgian trumpeters once boarded an open train car as an early way of testing the Doppler effect?

Or how about the fact that the single greatest death toll from the loss of a ship in the history of the US Navy is attributed by some people to the Bermuda Triangle?

Welcome to *THE BOOK FOR MEN WHO HAVE EVERYTHING* —a captivating compendium of facts, stories, anecdotes, tall tales, and games, all intended to expand the mind of the guy who— apparently—knows it all already...

This book is divided into 12 subject-based chapters, covering everything from movies to famous people, natural history to music, and sports to inventions. Inside each chapter, you'll find a fascinating mixture of dozens of stories, facts, and did-you-knows, each relating to the topic at hand. Along the way, you'll find stories about Thomas Edison, the gods of Greece and Rome, the Loch Ness monster, and a laboratory accident that improved car safety forever. (You'll even find out what tattoos, saunas, and boondocks have in common...)

Oh, and also included are a handful of matching games, trivia quizzes, and boredom-busting riddles for you to pit your wits against, too (as well as their solutions).

How you tackle all of this is up to you, of course. You can dive right in and simply turn the page to start expanding your mind in the field of movie-making, or else you can flick through the contents page, track down a topic that interests you, and dip into it however you choose!

Either way, hopefully everything here will be (mentally, at least) surplus to everything you already have!

MOVIES

MOVIE MILESTONES

◆ The first movie to earn $1 billion at the box office was James Cameron's *Titanic* in 1997, which reached a ten-figure gross on March 1, 1998, just 74 days after its release. Since then, there have been more than 50 billion-dollar movies in Hollywood, including Tim Burton's *Alice in Wonderland* in 2010, the 23rd James Bond movie, *Skyfall*, and both *The Dark Knight* and *The Dark Knight Rises*. In 2019, meanwhile, *Avengers: Endgame* earned the first billion dollars of its eventual $2.7 billion gross in just five days, setting the record for the fastest $1 billion gross in cinema history.

◆ In 1927, Al Jolson's *The Jazz Singer* famously became the first "talkie" in movie history when Jolson famously exclaimed, "You ain't heard nothin' yet!" In technical terms, a talkie is a full-length movie with synchronized sound and images, replacing the interspersed text cards of the previous silent movies. There had been a handful of short films prior to *The Jazz Singer* that used small amounts of synchronized sound, but Jolson's film was the first feature-length sound production.

◆ The world's first animated movie was the French short *Un bon bock* (A Good German Beer) by an early cinema pioneer named Émile Reynaud. Reynaud hand-painted the film's 700 picture cells in 1888, but the movie was not exhibited to the public until four year later, using his patented Théâtre Optique, or "optical theater"—an early example of a kind of projector known as a praxinoscope. The film told the story of a traveler who enters a rural cabaret club and orders a beer from a beautiful young waitress. While he attempts to court her, a kitchenhand enters the frame and surreptitiously drinks the man's beer.

◆ Actress Mary Pickford was the first person to sign a $1 million contract in Hollywood, albeit for a six-picture deal way back in 1916. The first person to sign a $1 million contract for a single movie was Marlon Brando, who was paid $1.25 million for his role as Fletcher Christian in *Mutiny on the Bounty* in 1962, and the first actress to negotiate a $1 million deal was Elizabeth Taylor in *Cleopatra*, the following year. More than two decades later, however, Brando became the first person in movie history to sign a $3 million contract for his role in *Superman*. He also negotiated a share of the movie's box office earnings and eventually earned more than $14 million (equivalent to almost $70 million today) for the film.

◆ The first film to face serious legal trouble was the famous German horror *Nosferatu* back in 1922. Legendary director F.W. Murnau's movie told the story of a vampire who seduces the wife of his realtor, and in the process brings a plague. It was clearly based on the 1897 novel *Dracula* by Bram Stoker, but Murnau had not acquired the rights to Stoker's story, and as a result, was sued by Stoker's widow for copyright violation. The resulting court order demanded Murnau destroy all copies of his film, but a handful survived. The movie has since gone on to be considered a masterpiece and set the template for the entire horror genre.

THE WORLD'S FIRST SCI-FI MOVIE

As modern a movie genre as it might seem, the very first science fiction movie in cinema history was actually made way back in 1902, by a French silent film pioneer named Georges Méliès.

Born in Paris in 1861, Méliès was working in the theater as a successful stage magician when he happened to see some of the earliest demonstrations of cinema—made by the famous Lumière Brothers—in 1895.

While the Lumières' films were brief real-life recordings of the likes of horse riders, busy streets, blacksmiths' workshops, and children playing, Méliès ingeniously saw the cinema as a potential extension of his work in the theater. Ultimately, he purchased a film camera, established a studio on the outskirts of Paris, and began building sets, designing costumes, hiring actors, and writing original narrative stories and screenplays for him and his co-stars to produce.

As a filmmaker, Méliès used his many years as a magician to incorporate clever camera tricks into his movies—playing with perspective and using double exposures, lighting techniques, and even stop-motion animation to bring his stories to life. He had early successes with a film adaptation of *Cinderella* in 1899 and a biographical retelling of the life of Joan of Arc (cinema's earliest biopic, no less!) in 1900, but Méliès' greatest success was *A Trip to the Moon*. It was a short silent film first shown in 1902, telling the story of a group of astronomers-turned-astronauts who board a rocket ship, travel into space, and land on the moon.

Incorporating fantastical elements of tales by authors such as Jules Verne and H.G. Wells, *A Trip to the Moon* continues with the astronomers encountering the moon goddess Selene, a cavern full of mushrooms, and bizarre alien creatures (played by dancers from Paris' Folies Bergère) who take the men captive below the lunar surface. The astronauts eventually manage to escape and flee back to Earth, where they are honored with a celebratory parade and a commemorative statue.

Despite being just eight minutes long, *A Trip to the Moon* has since earned its rightful place in movie history as the very first original science fiction film. The famous shot of the astronauts' smoking rocket ship crash-landed into the face of the Man in the Moon, meanwhile, has become one of the most iconic images of the silent era—and of the history of cinema itself. Appropriately enough, the Man in the Moon in the film was played by Méliès himself!

AWARDS SEASON

◆ One of the strangest glitches in Oscar history took place in 1945, when Hollywood actor Barry Fitzgerald received two nominations for exactly the same performance. Fitzgerald had starred opposite Bing Crosby in the religious comedy drama *Going My Way*, for which he was nominated for both Best Actor and Best Supporting Actor; Crosby, meanwhile, earned himself a lead actor nomination too. Thankfully, the Academy was saved the embarrassment of a single performer taking two Oscars home for the same role as Crosby took the Actor award, and Fitzgerald the Supporting Actor award—and the rules on category eligibility were changed the following year to prevent any similar overlap ever again!

◆ Barbra Streisand and Katharine Hepburn famously tied in the race for the Best Actress Oscar in 1969 for their roles in *Funny Girl* (Streisand's movie debut) and *The Lion in Winter*, respectively. This was Hepburn's third Best Actress award following *Morning Glory* in 1934 and *Guess Who's Coming to Dinner* in 1968. Given that she had won the previous year, it was presumed that Hepburn would not win again in 1969, but the two performers received exactly the same number of votes from the Academy's 3,030 members.

◆ Originally, the rules surrounding a tie at the Oscars stated that any two or more people or pictures that received within three votes of one another would be considered a tie. As a result, the first tie in Oscar history actually happened in the Best Actor race way back in 1932, when Fredric March (nominated for *Dr. Jekyll and Mr. Hyde*) and Wallace Beery (for *The Champ*) ended up splitting the award, despite Beery actually receiving one less vote than March!

◆ When *E.T.* and *Indiana Jones* composer John Williams was nominated for his work on the score to *Star Wars: The Rise of Skywalker* at the 2020 Academy Awards, he became the first (and to date, only) individual nominated for an Oscar in a staggering seven consecutive decades. Incredibly, Williams' first nomination was for *The Valley of the Dolls* way back in 1968, and he has maintained a steady flow of nominations every decade since.

◆ Greer Garson gave such a long and effusive speech after winning the Academy Award for Best Actress in *Mrs. Miniver* that the rules were changed in the aftermath to limit speakers' time on stage. Now capped at 45 seconds (with the odd exception here and there over the years), Garson's speech back in 1943 ran on for over six minutes before she left the stage.

◆ Whereas Best Actress winner Vivien Leigh clocked two hours and 23 minutes of screen time in *Gone with the Wind*, the shortest amount of time an Oscar-winning performance has spent on screen is just five minutes. Beatrice Straight won the 1976 Supporting Actress award for her performance as a wife confronting her unfaithful husband in *Network*; although she appears in a handful of shots in the movie, the majority of her performance consists of a single scene.

◆ Other performers who have received Oscars for notably brief screen times include Anthony Hopkins (who spent just under 25 minutes on screen as Hannibal Lecter in *The Silence of the*

Lambs), Jack Palance in *City Slickers* (on screen just under 12 and a half minutes), and Judi Dench (who spent just under six minutes on screen as Elizabeth I in *Shakespeare in Love*).

◆ At the 2nd Academy Awards ceremony in 1930 (honoring the movies of 1928 and 1929), there were just seven categories— Outstanding Picture, Director, Actor, Actress, Writing, Art Direction, and Cinematography—reduced from 12 in the previous year. Uniquely, each category in 1930 was won by a different movie, with no film taking more than one Oscar home that night—something that has never been repeated at any Oscar ceremony since.

◆ Given that each film received just one Oscar back in 1930, the Outstanding Picture winner that night, *The Broadway Melody*, became the first of only three films in the awards' history to win Oscar night's biggest prize and nothing else. Only 1932's *Grand Hotel* and 1935's *Mutiny on the Bounty* have ever done the same.

THE STORIES BEHIND
THE STUNTS

◆ In a now-famous scene in the 1973 Bond movie *Live and Let Die*, Bond (Roger Moore) finds himself trapped on a tiny island surrounded by crocodiles and runs across the creatures' backs as they lurk in the muddy water around him, using them as stepping stones to reach dry land. Incredibly, the stunt was filmed precisely as it appears on screen—with a series of live crocodiles, positioned in a row, and stuntman Ross Kananga sprinting across their backs before they have a chance to attack! Kananga was a crocodile farmer by trade, and it was on his farm that the shot was filmed. The crocodiles were tied and weighted down to the bottom of their pond to limit their movement, but their jaws and tails were left free to make it seem that they were not. Kananga took five takes to run successfully across the crocs' backs, at one point slipping into the water alongside them. In another famous outtake, he almost lost a foot when he slipped leaping from the last animal, and it closed its jaws around his shoe! For his remarkable efforts, Kananga was rewarded with not only one of the most courageous stunts in Bond history, but by being immortalized in the movie's script: the name of the film's villain, Mr. Big, was changed to Dr. Kananga in his honor!

◆ Michelle Pfeiffer's Catwoman in *Batman Returns* is one of the most iconic villains in cinema history. Although she had a stunt double for several of Catwoman's more acrobatic maneuvers in the film, in a now-famous scene in which Catwoman uses a whip to decapitate a series of mannequins in a storefront, it was Pfeiffer herself who was wielding it. After she successfully knocked the head off the fourth and final dummy (and then used the whip as a skipping rope to skip away nonchalantly), behind the cameras, the crew erupted into cheers and a spontaneous round of applause—an outtake that has since gone viral on YouTube.

◆ In a scene in *The Exorcist* in which the possessed daughter Regan (Linda Blair) uses her newfound supernatural powers to hurl her mother (Ellen Burstyn) across the room, it was Burstyn herself who was strapped into a retractable harness, designed to haul her at speed away from Regan's bed. Unfortunately, the harness was too powerful and pulled Burstyn to the ground so quickly that she fractured her coccyx.

◆ While filming the serial killer drama *Se7en*, Brad Pitt fell awkwardly during a rainy chase scene and broke his arm when it went through the windshield of a car. When the injury threatened to derail the already troubled production, director David Fincher decided to write Pitt's broken arm into the script, and he is seen with his arm in a sling in several scenes afterwards. Unfortunately, because the movie was not filmed sequentially, several scenes from before Pitt's character's injury had to be filmed in such a way that Pitt's actual injury was kept out of shot!

◆ Sylvester Stallone opted to perform several of the stunts in his debut Rambo movie, *First Blood*, himself. In one memorable scene in which Rambo leaps from a cliff and injures himself striking off tree branches on the way down, Stallone performed the final third of the fall himself—and broke a rib striking a tree branch on the way down!

◆ Steve McQueen was such a talented motorcyclist that he proved a better driver than his stunt driver in the World War II drama *The Great Escape* and ultimately ended up filming much of the famous final chase himself. In one sequence of shots, in fact, McQueen dressed as the German soldier pursuing his character through open countryside and so is chasing after himself! The famous climactic 60-foot motorcycle jump, however, was deemed too dangerous for even McQueen to attempt (despite his protests that he could manage it), and so for insurance reasons, legendary stunt rider Bud Ekins took to the saddle in his place.

◆ 1992 horror movie *The Candyman* memorably featured a villain who could spew live bees onto his victims. Unfortunately for actor Tony Todd, the bees were very real, and 200,000 of them were used in the production. Wisely, however, Todd negotiated a clause in his contract that awarded him an extra $1,000 fee for every bee sting he received during production; he eventually walked away with an extra $23,000.

HOW HITCHCOCK MADE SHOWERS SCARY

The murder of Marion Crane in the shower in Alfred Hitchcock's 1960 thriller *Psycho* is easily now one of the most famous (if not infamous) scenes in the history of horror cinema.

Hitchcock revealed in a 1972 interview with Dick Cavett that in preparation for the scene, the prop department at the MGM studios built him a fake rubber torso, fitted inside with tubes of fake blood that would squirt out when struck with a knife. But at no point in the scene is the killer's knife ever seen cutting Janet Leigh's character, and despite the prop department's efforts, the rubber torso went unused. Instead, Hitchcock filmed the scene in such a way that most of the scene's violence is kept squarely in the viewer's imagination.

According to movie legend (and Hitchcock himself), the *Psycho* shower scene required a total of 78 camera setups, each shooting from a different angle and at a different distance from Leigh's and the killer's points of view. These different shots were then rapidly spliced together, disorienting the viewer and giving the knife attack itself a terrifyingly frenetic energy. The 45-second sequence ultimately took almost a week to film, from December 17 to 23, 1959 (with the scene further delayed while Leigh recovered from a cold).

Some of the shots were easier to accomplish than others. The final shot of the sequence, in which a close-up of Marion's eye slowly fades into a close-up of the shower plughole, required several retakes as the spray from the water kept making Leigh blink (notwithstanding the logistics of rotating and pulling the camera away while maintaining focus). Likewise, Hitchcock's desire to have a shot of the water pouring down from the showerhead straight at the camera necessitated some particularly fiendish camera trickery and on-set ingenuity: as keen-eyed viewers will be able to spot, the central holes in the showerhead are actually blocked, so that no water sprays out of them, providing a dry spot beneath it in which the camera could be placed. The shot of Marion's blood being washed away, however, was far easier to film. Given that the movie was made in black and white (a decision Hitchcock reportedly made due to a smaller-than-expected budget, not for any artistic reasons), the blood is actually Hershey's chocolate syrup!

CUT! SCENES THAT ENDED UP ON THE CUTTING ROOM FLOOR

◆ David Cronenberg's 1986 body horror *The Fly* features a scene in which the scientist David Brundle (Jeff Goldblum) successfully transports a baboon from one teleportation pod to another (following an earlier unsuccessful attempt, in which the baboon is turned inside out). A cut scene from the same movie, however, pushed its notorious gruesomeness even further: Brundle places a baboon and a cat in two separate pods, and then watches as the two are unintentionally morphed together to create a hideous monkey-cat hybrid that proceeds to attack him in suitably bloody style. The scene proved too much even for *The Fly* and ended up on the cutting room floor.

◆ The 1933 version of *King Kong* originally featured a scene in which the explorers of Kong's home, Skull Island, fall into a chasm and are gradually picked off by a series of insects, giant spiders, and reptiles. Allegedly, the producers at RKO deemed the sequence too gruesome for the final cut and demanded it be removed from the film; other accounts claim the sequence was shown to preview audiences, who responded by fainting, screaming, and running from the theater. Whatever the truth, the sequence never made it into the final movie (although it was revived in suitably gruesome fashion by Peter Jackson in his 2005 remake).

◆ The final cut of *Harry Potter and the Deathly Hallows: Part 1* originally included a scene in which Harry's cousin, Dudley, finally makes peace with him, shakes his hand, and tells him outside their family home, "I don't think you're a waste of space." Despite bringing some closure to Harry's troubled homelife and the pair's uncomfortable relationship, the 20-second scene was cut from the final film.

◆ In a now-famous two-minute deleted scene from James Cameron's *Aliens*, Ripley, played by Sigourney Weaver, is seen mourning a daughter she has left behind on Earth. Despite the scene giving important context to Ripley's ultimate adoption of the young child Newt in the film, the scene was considered too slow and too emotional to stand out against the nonstop action in the rest of the movie and ended up on the cutting room floor.

◆ In a famous deleted scene from the acclaimed thriller *The Silence of the Lambs*, FBI agent Clarice Starling (Jodie Foster) pays an additional visit to Hannibal Lecter (Anthony Hopkins) in his cell to find out more details about the serial killer Buffalo Bill. After some more *quid pro quo*, Lecter gives Clarice a few more clues to Bill's identity and begins to tear up as he describes Bill's troubled childhood and the "years of systematic abuse" that turned him into a killer. The tense and dramatic scene—consisting of a two-minute *tour de force* monologue by Hopkins—is played out in such a way that the audience is left wondering how much of Lecter's description is of Bill and how much of it is of his own past. However powerful the scene may have been, it proved a step too far in humanizing Lecter and ended up being cut from the final movie.

A POTTED HISTORY OF CGI

S pecial effects have been a part of the movies since the days of silent film, but it's only since the 1970s that directors have been able to use imagery and effects generated by computer programs to bring their most outlandish and spectacular ideas to life on screen.

◆ The first mainstream use of what we would now recognize as CGI filmmaking was in the 1973 adaptation of *Westworld*, directed by future *Jurassic Park* author Michael Crichton. The movie featured Yul Brynner as an android, with 2D pixelated computer-generated effects used to replicate his point of view on the screen. The 1976 sequel *Futureworld* pushed the technology even further, to render 3D computer-generated effects on screen.

◆ CGI use remained fairly limited in movies throughout the 1970s, but the following decade was different. *Tron* in 1982 used computer-generated imagery to create entire sets and environments on screen, implementing groundbreaking techniques to cast real actors into entire CGI surroundings. The following year, *Star Trek* sequel *The Wrath of Khan* used similar techniques to create the landscapes of alien planets.

◆ In 1985, Barry Levinson's *Young Sherlock Holmes* featured a scene in which a stained-glass knight leaps from a window frame in a church and attacks a priest. The CGI knight is credited with being the first fully rendered, entirely computer-generated character in movie history.

◆ Walt Disney's *The Great Mouse Detective* provided another milestone in 1986, when computer-generated wireframe models of the gears inside a giant clock were used alongside traditional cel animation to bring the film's climactic battle inside Big Ben to the screen. This was the first predominantly computer-generated scene in Disney's history and the first time such techniques had been combined on screen.

◆ Animated movies again pushed CGI further in 1995, with *Toy Story*—the first entirely computer-generated movie in history. The 81-minute film was a global blockbuster, earning more than ten times its somewhat meager $30 million budget at the box office.

◆ Actor Andy Serkis played the entirely CGI character Gollum in Peter Jackson's *Lord of the Rings* trilogy, with a series of groundbreaking CGI techniques used to bring the character to life. The filmmakers not only combined traditional CGI animation and motion capturing (that is, recording Serkis' performance using a specialized suit) but also invented a new technique dubbed 'rotoanimation' that laboriously replaced Serkis' image in the film with a digitally rendered Gollum.

◆ Cinema's first entirely motion-captured animated film was Robert Zemeckis' *The Polar Express* in 2004. The film's stars—including Tom Hanks—performed the film wearing special motion-capturing suits, with recordings of their movements then fed into a computer to form the basis of the computer-generated characters. The same technology was then used, in an improved and far more detailed way, in James Cameron's *Avatar* in 2009, which used even more detailed motion-capture techniques to pick up on the slightest movements of the actors' eyes, mouths, and faces.

THE MGM LIONS

From the Paramount Studios mountain (merely a fictional peak, not an actual place) to Columbia Pictures' Lady with the Lamp (a personification of America, originally modeled on the silent movie actress Doris Doscher), all the biggest studios have assured themselves a place in film history with memorable and instantly recognizable logos. And perhaps the most dramatic of all of them all is the roaring lion of MGM.

Metro-Goldwyn-Mayer's lion logo was the brainchild of the studio's original chief publicist, Howard Dietz, who lifted the idea from the lion mascot of his alma mater, Columbia University. Introduced to the studio's film in 1924, the very first MGM lion was silent. Footage recorded of a lion named Slats was placed inside the studio's iconic film-reel logo, but originally, all Slats did was sit in silence and look around.

It wasn't until the advent of sound that a roaring lion appeared in the MGM logo for the first time in 1928. By now, however, Slats had retired, and so a new lion—another male named Jackie, who had been captured in Sudan and then trained in captivity in America—was brought in to replace him. Although sound was now a firm fixture of MGM Movies, Jackie's footage was filmed silently, and his roar was then dubbed over the footage. At least four different recordings of Jackie's roar were used over the next three decades.

As filmmakers began to experiment with different kinds of media, color film, and aspect ratios over the subsequent decades, MGM was forced to update its logo several times so that it matched the appearance of whatever film that followed it. Ultimately, a series of different lions named Bill, Telly, Tanner, George, and Coffee all made varying numbers of appearances at the start of MGM movies from the 1930s to the late 1960s. The longest-serving lion in this era was Tanner, whose footage was used before all Technicolor MGM films from 1934 to 1956 (and all MGM animations until 1967). The recording of his roar, meanwhile, became a stock sound effect used long afterwards.

The eighth and final MGM lion, named Leo, made his debut appearance before the drama *Tip on a Dead Jockey* in 1957 and remains in use to this day—albeit with a series of tweaks over the decades. Originally seen to be roaring three times, Leo's logo was cut down to just two in 1960. Then, in the early 1980s, Leo's roar (which was actually recorded from Tanner) was replaced by the work of Oscar-winning sound engineer Mark Mancini, who ditched the lion altogether and used a tiger's roar instead. The redubbed and rerecorded footage made its debut before *Poltergeist* in 1982.

In the 21st century, MGM has once again embraced more modern technology, with Leo's image digitally restored in 2008 and replaced with a CGI-animated lion, modeled on Leo, in 2021.

THE TEN MOST EXPENSIVE MOVIES OF ALL TIME

Filmmaking can be an expensive business, with costs often spiraling out of control and post-production and promotion frequently inflating a film's budget even after the cameras have stopped rolling. Not only that, but as inflation has changed over time, comparing one movie's cost to another's is a notoriously tricky business: 1963's *Cleopatra*, starring Elizabeth Taylor, cost $31 million in '60s terms, but would be more than ten times that much today! Based on the final declared dollar fee, unadjusted for inflation—and excluding trilogies and other multiple productions filmed concurrently—as of the 2020s, the ten most expensive films of all time are:

◆◆ 1 ◆◆

Star Wars: The Force Awakens (2015)
$447 million

◆◆ 2 ◆◆

Jurassic World: Fallen Kingdom (2018)
$432 million

◆◆ 3 ◆◆

Star Wars: The Rise of Skywalker (2019)
$416 million

4

Fast X (2023)
$379 million

5

Pirates of the Caribbean: On Stranger Tides (2011)
$379 million

6

Avengers: Age of Ultron (2015)
$365 million

7

Avengers: Endgame (2019)
$356 million

8

Doctor Strange in the Multiverse of Madness (2022)
$351 million

9

Avatar: The Way of Water (2022)
$350 million

10

Ant-Man and the Wasp: Quantumania (2023)
$330 million

BOREDOM BUSTERS 1

What can you catch, but not throw?

◆ ◆

I can travel around the world without ever leaving my corner.
What am I?

◆ ◆

When A was eight, B was half his age. Now A is 14.
How old is B?

◆ ◆

What animal can you make a toga out of?

◆ ◆

What can you put between one and two to make a figure higher
than one but lower than two?

(Find solutions on page 196.)

INVENTIONS
& TECHNOLOGY

ACCIDENTAL INVENTIONS

◆ At the 1904 St. Louis World Fair, ice cream vendor Arnold Fornachou was selling so much of his product that he ran out of paper cups in which to serve it. Meanwhile, at a nearby stall, vendor Ernest Hamwi was struggling to find an audience for his brittle, fritter-like Middle Eastern waffle cakes, called zalabia. Sensing an opportunity to combine forces, Fornachou began serving his ice cream inside Hamwi's waffles, and in doing so invented the ice cream cone.

◆ In 1844, New York dentist Horace Wells was at a party when one of the guests—entertaining themselves by getting high on nitrous oxide, or "laughing gas"—fell and suffered a terrible cut to their leg. To Wells' surprise, the party guest felt nothing. Seeing an opportunity to relieve his patients' discomfort, Wells arranged for an experiment in which he took a dose of nitrous oxide himself, then had a fellow dentist pull a rotten tooth from his mouth. When he came to, Wells had indeed suffered no pain from the procedure and began advocating for the use of anesthesia in dental practices. Although his story ends ignominiously (a public demonstration of his theory was a disaster, and having left the profession under a cloud, he took his own life in 1848), the American Dental Association soon recognized that he had been right all along and attributed the invention of dental anesthesia to him in 1864.

◆ In the mid-1930s, researchers at DuPont began horsing around with a flask containing an unusual liquid polymer that could be drawn out into long strands using a glass stirrer. As a game, the scientists began trying to make the longest strands they could, even going so far as to run down the corridors of their laboratories without the strand snapping. Before long, however, it dawned on them that by stretching the liquid out like this, they could intentionally convert it into solid threads, which could then be spun and woven. Their game ultimately led to the invention of nylon, the world's first synthetic fabric.

◆ In 1968, a researcher named Spencer Silver was attempting to make a super-strong adhesive in the laboratories of the 3M company in Minnesota, when he unintentionally invented the complete opposite: an adhesive so weak that it barely held anything together and could be easily separated, leaving no trace of its stickiness behind. Thinking nothing more of his apparent failure, Silver shelved his invention, and it sat unused for the next five years. Then, in 1973, a colleague of Silver's saw some potential in Silver's weak glue—he had found it difficult to keep his place in his church hymnbook. Using the glue to make adhesive paper bookmarks, the duo inadvertently invented the Post-It note.

HOW TO BUILD A
SUSPENSION BRIDGE

From the Golden Gate to England's immense Humber crossing, suspension bridges are some of the most extraordinary structures in the engineering world. Even more incredibly, they're also some of the oldest. The origins of the modern suspension bridge can be traced back to the first millennium BCE, when so-called "simple suspension" or catenary bridges began to emerge across China, Tibet, and central Asia.

This early kind of cabled crossing—which was also developed in the pre-contact Americas—involved the use of ropes, vines, or, later, metal chains that were simply suspended across a river or gorge from one side to the other. Originally, people would simply have walked across the ropes themselves, but over time, boards were added to form makeshift walkways, suspended in the air by the taut ropes and cables above.

Modern suspension bridges, however, are far more complex and often utilize immense towers that both further the bridge's span and lift its load-bearing cables many hundreds of feet into the air. But no matter how large a suspension bridge may be (and typically, they're the largest and longest crossings in the world today), the principle behind them has remained the same since ancient times.

The crossing surface of the bridge (i.e., the road) is, as its name suggests, suspended from the cables above it. The long, curved, upper cables of a suspension bridge are called the mains, and the vertical cables that link them to the road below are called the suspenders. At either end of the bridge, heavy, deep-set anchorages hold down the opposite ends of the main cables, keeping them taut enough to support the cables suspended from them, and in turn the road below.

Building a bridge of this kind is understandably complex. Typically, the first stage involves creating the enormous bases of the towers, known as piers, which often need to be built deep into the ground or riverbed below. When building the Brooklyn Bridge in the late 1800s, workers known as "sandhogs" beavered away inside gigantic hollow structures, called caissons, working at such depths that they had to have oxygen pumped inside them. Conditions were so harsh that many sandhog workers ended the day with a case of the bends (or decompression sickness).

With these supporting piers in place, the anchorages can be built at either end of the bridge and fitted with so-called "eye-bars," to which the main cables can be attached. The cables themselves are now typically made of thousands of individual steel wires, interwound with one another to provide extra strength, like the individual fibers of a rope. With these cables in place, the suspenders can be laid in place, and the roadway built beneath them.

Despite their solid structure and ability to support immense weights, suspension bridges are often so large that they are notoriously susceptible to adverse weather conditions. Consequently, they have to be built in such a way that they can warp in heat and move in storms without the cables breaking or the roadway rupturing. Incredibly, engineers are now able to work this into the structure itself, so that a bridge many hundreds of feet tall, and capable of bearing many hundreds of thousands of tons of weight, can sway back and forth with the wind!

QUIZ: EPONYMOUS INVENTIONS

Of the 16 inventions listed below, 12 of them are named after their inventor or discoverer. The other four are red herrings. Which is which?

Mason jar	Bunsen burner
Stetson hat	Trilby hat
Petri dish	Catherine wheel
Ferris wheel	Diesel engine
Jacuzzi	Bakelite plastic
Saxophone	Trombone
Biro pen	Zamboni
Rubik's cube	Khaki fatigues

(Find solutions on page 196.)

SEEING IT THROUGH: THE INVENTION OF X-RAYS

I t was Professor Wilhelm Roentgen, working at the physics department of the University of Wurzburg, in Bavaria, who discovered X-rays way back in 1895. Since then, they have become an increasingly commonplace means of diagnosing everything from broken bones and fractures to infected teeth and digestive troubles in dogs! But Professor Roentgen's discovery all those years ago was, incredibly, a complete accident.

Roentgen had been studying fluorescence and was working on an experiment to see if cathode rays could pass through solid glass vacuum tubes. The cathode ray tube that he was working with was wrapped in a protective covering of thick black card—so it was unusual that it appeared to project an eerie greenish glow onto a nearby piece of light-sensitive fluorescent paper.

From this initial observation, Roentgen began experimenting further to see what else, if anything, the rays appeared to be able to pass through. To his surprise, they seemed to be able to pass through all but the most solid of objects—including human flesh, though they seemed unable to pass through bone. Roentgen tested out this final discovery by using his cathode tube and fluorescent paper to take a photograph of the bones of his wife's hand.

Unable to discern quite yet what this so-called "invisible light" was, Roentgen named these penetrative rays "x-rays"—x having long been used to symbolize the unknown.

As news of his discovery spread, and its applications in medicine became increasingly clear, Roentgen soon became the talk of the scientific community and was honored with the very first Nobel Prize for Physics in 1901.

INVENTIONS THAT ARE OLDER THAN THEY SEEM

◆ The world's first automatic vending machine was a coin-operated holy water dispenser, invented by Hero of Alexandria way back in the 1st century CE. When a coin was deposited through a slot at the top of the machine, it landed on a tilting pan that would open a valve inside and dispense a small amount of water.

◆ The printing press arrived in Europe in the early 1400s, and from there spread to England and eventually across the Atlantic to America. The technique of using movable type to print multiple copies of books and documents, however, is even older than that: although the use of movable type was later perfected in Korea in the 1300s, the oldest printed book in the world is the Diamond Sutra, produced in China in 888 CE.

◆ Plastic drinking straws might be a 20th-century invention, but the idea of sipping up a drink through a tube is an ancient one: the Sumerians are known to have used hollow reeds as drinking straws around 7,000 years ago.

◆ Although the modern whoopee cushion was invented in Canada in 1930, you can thank the Roman child emperor Elagabalus for coming up with the idea way back in the third century. According to contemporary reports, 14-year-old Elagabalus—the youngest emperor in Rome's history—liked to place inflated bladders beneath the cushions of his chairs so that they emitted bizarre noises and slowly lowered the guests beneath the height of the table as they sat down to eat.

◆ You likely haven't heard of a yakhchaal, but you no doubt have the equivalent to this ancient Asian invention in your kitchen. Originating in ancient Persia around 400 BC, a yakhchaal is a vaguely cone-shaped structure that worked as a refrigerator to store and produce ice. Although the precise design of the structure changed from region to region, most worked by harnessing the action of so-called evaporative cooling to keep the air inside the yakhchaal cool enough for ice to be stored even in the warmest desert areas.

THE FIRST WORD SENT OVER THE INTERNET

These days, we take the ability to write and send messages remotely for granted. The average person, for instance, will send just over six million messages in their lifetime—and a whopping 23 billion text messages alone are sent around the world every single day. Back in the early days of the internet, however, sending even one word was oddly problematic.

It was way back in the autumn of 1969 that early computer engineers working on the ARPANET (a precursor to the modern internet) at UCLA were trying to figure out how to use this new remote communications technology to send a message from one university campus to another. After a considerable amount of tinkering with their system, at around nine o'clock in the evening on October 29, UCLA professor Leonard Kleinrock and his student Charley Kline were finally ready to try the first transmission, relaying an online message from their campus to Stanford, a few hundred miles away. Their test word was to be a typically on-theme one: LOGIN.

Unfortunately, midway through the test, something all computer users will be familiar with happened: the system crashed. The first message ever sent over the internet, ultimately, was nothing more than the two letters "LO." It took another hour or so before the full five-letter word, LOGIN, was successfully sent over the ARPANET and, at 10:30 pm that evening, a new world of communication was born.

HOW A KITCHEN ERROR GAVE US CORN FLAKES

T he Kellogg's breakfast cereal company is named after two American brothers, John Harvey and Will Keith Kellogg, who worked together at a sanitarium in Battle Creek, Michigan, in the late 1800s.

The pair used their restorative clinic as a backdrop for faddish health treatments, such as hydrotherapy (which back then involved little more than taking baths at different temperatures) and a strict dietary and exercise regimen the pair called "biological living." Long before the true content of many of our foods was fully appreciated, digestive complaints and dyspepsia were endemic in the American population, and the Kelloggs believed that a blander, plainer, grain-based diet was the key to relieving the pain.

The kitchens at the brothers' Battle Creek resort were ultimately used as much for experimentation as they were for preparing food for the clinic's patients. But one day, one of the brothers accidentally left a newly mixed batch of grain-based dough out on a kitchen countertop, inadvertently allowing it to dry and partially ferment overnight. The following day, when the dough was rolled out, it splintered into dozens of individual flakes.

Not wanting to waste it, the brothers baked it anyway—and the result was a hearty and healthy batch of baked corn flakes.

THERE'S A FIRST TIME FOR EVERYTHING:

UNSUCCESSFUL TRIAL RUNS OF INVENTIONS

◆ Franz Reichelt was an Austrian-born French inventor and tailor who developed his own design for a parachute. Having earlier tested his prototype by flinging mannequins out of his fifth-floor apartment window, Reichelt petitioned the Parisian authorities to allow him to test out his parachute from a greater height and set his sights on the Eiffel Tower. Finally allowed to utilize the tower on an icy morning in February 1912, Reichelt made the inadvisable decision not to use a mannequin this time, but to test his parachute himself before a stunned crowd of spectators. He leapt from the first platform, but sadly, the chute failed to open effectively, and Reichelt fatally struck the frozen ground below.

◆ In 1903, a 24-year-old General Electric employee named William Nelson decided to take a new invention out for a test drive. He had been working on a newly motorized bicycle and had produced a prototype model of his own design. Unfortunately, while on his test drive, Nelson fell from the speedy bicycle while riding up a hill near Mapleton, New York, and was killed instantly. In a bizarre coincidence, the hillside overlooked the home of his father-in-law.

◆ A famous (and perhaps apocryphal) Chinese tale tells of a gentleman named Wan Hu in the 16th century, who intended to travel into space by strapping rockets to his chair. Once lit, the 47 rockets all exploded, killing him instantly.

◆ One of the earliest recorded aviation pioneers was an 11th-century Turkic scholar (and author of one of the earliest dictionaries of Arabic) named Ismail ibn Hammad al-Jawhari. Way back in 1010 CE, al-Jawhari took it upon himself to test heavier-than-air flight by attaching two wooden wings to his arms and leaping from the roof of a mosque in the Iranian city of Nishapur. Sadly (though perhaps predictably), his invention failed to support his weight, and al-Jawhari fell to his death.

◆ In 1753, Russian–German physicist Georg Wilhelm Richmann built an early kind of lightning rod as part of a larger apparatus of his own design with which he intended to study electricity. Unfortunately, in a test operation conducted during an immense electrical storm, Richmann's device produced a ball of lightning inside his home laboratory that fired outwards into the room, struck him in the forehead, and killed him instantly.

TOP TEN: MOST IMPORTANT INVENTIONS

In 2017, the British cultural and historical organization English Heritage surveyed its members to find out what they considered to be the most important inventions of all time. The results were as follows:

◆◆ **1** ◆◆

Wheel

◆◆ **2** ◆◆

Fridge

◆◆ **3** ◆◆

Sewerage and sanitation systems

◆◆ **4** ◆◆

Plow

◆◆ **5** ◆◆

Penicillin

◆◆ **6** ◆◆

The Internet

◆◆ **7** ◆◆

Armor

◆◆ **8** ◆◆

Light bulb

◆◆ **9** ◆◆

Clock

◆◆ **10** ◆◆

Tea bags

BOREDOM BUSTERS 2

What kind of room is only big enough to put your feet in?

◆ ◆

What three consecutive numbers give the same result, no matter whether they're added or multiplied together?

◆ ◆

What country is the easiest to break?

◆ ◆

What animal do you get if you add the back end of a horse to the front end of an alpaca?

◆ ◆

What word gets shorter when you add two extra letters to it?

(Find solutions on page 196.)

WORLD HISTORY

UNUSUAL BATTLES
AND WARS

◆ In medieval times, it was by no means unusual for kings, princes, and other rulers to lead their own troops into battle themselves. However, a legendary battle charge led by Luxembourg's King John of Bohemia at the Battle of Crécy in 1346 has gone down in history as one of the most unusual, as John had lost his sight. It was a decade earlier, while crusading in Lithuania, that King John is believed to have gone blind, perhaps as the result of a genetic condition, or according to other accounts, as a result of some kind of plague or similar infection. Either way, by the time he tethered his horse to that of one of his fellow fighters and joined the French in a last-ditch assault on the English at Crécy, King John would not have been able to see what lay ahead. Despite his boldness and bravery, unfortunately, John was killed in the battle—ironically, according to yet another account of the day's fighting, by having a blade thrust into his eye.

◆ An island group off the Indian Ocean coast of what is now Tanzania, Zanzibar was a strategically important location in the days of colonial trade. As a result, when the pro-British sultan of Zanzibar, Hamad bin Thuwaini, died in 1896, it was in Britain's interests to ensure his replacement held similarly sympathetic views. However, the sultan's cousin, Khalid ibn Barghash, had other ideas. Rumored to have poisoned the sultan himself, the decidedly anti-British Khalid quickly assumed power, instantly putting Britain's trade interests in the region in peril. The British consequently issued an ultimatum: Khalid had 24 hours to step

◆◆◆

down or else they would declare war. The ensuing Anglo–Zanzibar war was declared at 9:02 a.m. on August 27—but the British so obviously outnumbered and out-armed Khalid and his supporters that the conflict came to an end just 38 minutes later. It remains the shortest war in history.

◆ In 1832, a French pastry chef known as Monsieur Remontel was working on the outskirts of Mexico City when his shop was looted by bandits and all his wares were stolen. Enraged by the lawlessness of the time, Remontel challenged the local government over the assault on his business and demanded they pay compensation for allowing such behavior to go on all but unchecked. When no compensation was paid, Remontel appealed to the French government to step in, which promptly demanded Mexico pay a staggering 600,000 pesos in reparations, both for Remontel's damages and others suffered by similar French-controlled businesses in the area. When again no money was paid, France embarked on a month-long assault on Mexican trading centers, barricading and blockading ports all along Mexico's east coast in what became known as the Pastry War. After a few weeks of skirmishes here and there, a peace treaty was eventually signed, and the French removed their ships from the ports—though Mexico never did end up paying the fee the French had demanded!

◆ In 1385, the Italian city-states of Bologna and Modena went to war over a bucket. A group of soldiers from Modena had earlier stolen the wooden pail from the main well in the center of nearby Bologna, some 25 miles to the east. In a rather uncompromising and disproportionate response, Bologna declared war on Modena and rallied around 30,000 troops to march on the city and retrieve

◆◆◆

the bucket. The only clash in the so-called War of the Oaken Bucket was the resultant Battle of Zappolino, fought in November 1385, in which the Bolognese were unceremoniously routed from Modena and pushed back to Bologna—with the forces from Modena not only keeping the bucket but also putting it proudly on display in their city's main bell tower—where it has remained ever since.

◆ On October 18, 1925, the neighboring Balkan nations of Greece and Bulgaria almost went to war with one another over a stray dog. The border between the two countries was hotly defended at the time, and as a result, any person—or in this case, any animal— that happened to cross it caused these local tensions to reach a boiling point. As a result, when a stray dog just so happened to wander from one country into the other, that was all that was needed for a firefight to break out across the border, ultimately threatening to throw the two mutually belligerent neighbors into a far larger frontier war. Luckily, the battle came to an end before too many shots were fired, and the War of the Stray Dog was over almost as soon as it began.

STRANGEST
KINGS & QUEENS

◆ Many ancient rulers and kings have suffered from various forms of madness, but perhaps one of the most unusual was the delusion of the medieval French king, Charles VI. He ruled over France for more than 40 years, from 1380 to 1422, during which time he became increasingly convinced that his entire body was made of glass. Terrified that any quick movement would surely cause him to shatter into thousands of pieces, Charles spent much of his life wrapped in blankets and padding, forbade any of his courtiers to touch him, and vowed never to go outside out of fear that one of the local glaziers would melt him down and turn him into a window.

◆ Zhu Houzhao, known as the Zhengde Emperor of Ming-era China, was a bizarrely capricious and deluded ruler whose outlandish behavior is considered by some historians to have begun the downfall of his entire dynasty. Assuming the throne at the age of just 14, Zhu Houzhao used his position to make numerous increasingly bizarre, wasteful, and time-consuming demands on his court and his people. Deciding he wanted to be a solider, for instance, he organized and led an excursion into Jiangxi province in an attempt to capture a local prince whom he had heard had dared to revolt against his authority; when the emperor arrived to find the man had already been caught, he ordered his release just so he could hunt him down and catch him again himself. In one of his most bizarre demands, however, Zhu Houzhao instructed his servants to deck out the halls of his palace to resemble a city market and act as local vendors so that he could safely wander the "streets" of his kingdom and experience life as an ordinary citizen without ever actually setting foot outside.

◆ Friedrich Wilhelm I ruled the grand European country of Prussia from 1713 to 1740. As king, he was obsessed with the military and would often personally drill his troops himself, sleep with them in their quarters, and even have them march before him when he was ill and confined to his bed. His obsession even affected his family: according to legend, Friedrich Wilhelm I was so intent on ensuring his son, Friedrich II, would be a model soldier that he had him woken every morning with a cannon blast to acclimatize him to the sound.

◆ Violently disapproving of his son Peter's choice of wife, the medieval king of Portugal, Alfonso IV, reportedly had his son's lover, Inês, assassinated in horrifically bloody fashion: three of his most loyal soldiers reportedly stormed the monastery in which the king had already had her detained and decapitated her in front of one of her children. Understandably, Inês' murder drove a deep wedge between Peter and his father, so that when he took to the throne as King Peter I after Alfonso's death in 1357, Peter tracked down his lovers' assassins and supposedly tore their hearts from their chests with his bare hands. Just when you thought this gruesome tale could not get any worse, however, by this time Peter had been driven so mad with grief that he demanded Inês' body be exhumed, dressed in royal regalia, and positioned in the queen's throne beside him so that they could rule together even after her death.

◆◆◆

◆ After the deaths of both his adoptive mother and grandmother within a matter of weeks of one another in 1757, Yi Seon, Crown Prince Sado of Korea, became increasingly and violently insane. At first, his madness led to him merely beating and thrashing the eunuchs and servants of his father King Yeongjo of Joseon's court, but over time, his wild attacks became more violent, and he would frequently murder his father's staff as a means of releasing even the merest of frustrations. He also developed an intense fear of wearing clothes, known as vestiphobia, and would have his servants burn his clothes, claiming they were inhabited by evil spirits. Eventually, when he began to turn his violent attacks against his family (he beat his consort Bing-ae to death in 1761 and was rumored to be planning to assassinate his father), the king was compelled to take action—albeit in a bizarrely macabre fashion. As the law forbade the body of any royal to be harmed or defiled in any way, making execution legally impossible, King Yeongjo had his son shut away inside a four-foot rice chest and left without food or water. According to palace reports, it took eight days for him to die.

HOW TO MAKE AN ENIGMA MACHINE

A way from the front line, one of the greatest non-combative moments of World War II was the Allies' cracking of the so-called Enigma code from their secret intelligence services' headquarters at Bletchley Park, England.

Enigma was the name given to the top-secret cipher used by Nazi Germany to encode their important strategic communications. To do so, they used an Enigma machine—a typewriter-like device that would transform any message typed into it into an ever-changing secret code. Breaking this code and understanding Germany's (and later, Japan's) use of the Enigma machine ultimately proved a significant turning point in the course of the war.

Invented in the Netherlands, Enigma machines were originally intended to be used to transmit confidential banking information, but in 1923, Germany purchased the patent from the Dutch and began to use the machines in their intelligence communications instead.

As luck would have it, however, Polish intelligence also happened to acquire an Enigma machine around this time, and having obtained an operator's codebook from a French secret agent, they quickly set about painstakingly breaking the German cipher. After Hitler invaded Poland in 1939, however, the Polish forces were compelled to send their work and equipment to the Allies out of fear that it would fall into the wrong hands—leaving it up to the Allies to crack the code instead.

On the surface, the Enigma system was fairly straightforward: the code itself was merely a substitution cipher (i.e., one letter of the alphabet randomly swapped for another), while the Enigma machines worked simply to replace one letter of a typed message at a time following this new randomized code. All a user had to do was check the instructions in their codebook to configure the workings of the machine in a certain way, and then, as they typed their message into the machine letter by letter, follow the uniquely coded version of it that would be illuminated on a bank of lettered lights above the keyboard. The sender would write down these letters as they went and then transmit the coded message, via Morse code, to their contact.

At the other end, the recipient merely had to set up their Enigma machine following the same configurations as the sender and then type the coded message into the keyboard. The decoded version would then be lit up, one letter at a time, by the illuminated letters. As simple a system as this might sound, however, the actual workings of the Enigma machine itself were astonishingly intricate, and four separate layers of encryption and complexity were incorporated into every single message.

First of all, there was the machine's plugboard—a bank of electronic connecting sockets, each marked by a letter, that worked a little like a telephone switchboard using wires to connect different letters of the alphabet. To set up the machine, a user would follow a series of instructions in the codebook to connect, say, the letter A to G, B to Q, C to J, and so on, instigating the first scramble of the message.

This arrangement of the cables on the plugboard changed each day, so if a code were to be solved today, it would be out of date tomorrow, and a whole new configuration of letter-connecting cables would have to be used 24 hours later. A second layer of complexity, however, lay in a series of gear-like removable rotors, fitted into slots inside the Enigma machine, around the edges of which were imprinted the 26 letters of the alphabet. There were up to five of these removable rotors in each Enigma machine, with a different arrangement of three of them required each day. So, as well as being instructed to link letter A to G and B to Q, and so on, a user would also be told to, say, place rotors #3, #5, and #2 inside the machine and set them to begin on, say, the letters D, W, and H.

A third layer of complexity was ensured by having these gears rotate a single step after each key on the keyboard was pressed, so that the D–W–H position would last for just one letter before the rotors changed position and the code was re-scrambled. As a result, the letters in the message were not only substituted but each successive letter was substituted by an entirely new configuration—so even two identical letters typed one after the other (such as "EE") would produce two non-identical letters (such as "TX") in the final message.

Lastly, a fourth and final level of complexity was ensured by utilizing an electronic reflector, which passed the initial coded signal through this internal system of scrambling connections for a second jumbling. So even though the user might connect A to G on the plugboard, typing the "G" signal then sent by plugboard when the user typed an A would first be scrambled by the rotors, then reflected and passed back through the rotors and back into the plugboard as a completely different letter, before this letter's signal was then sent from the plugboard through the rotors

and onto the illuminated board. The rotors would then change position, and an entirely new configuration would click into place for the next letter.

With so many moving parts, reflected connections, and multiple layers of complexity, there were a staggering 150 million million million possible solutions to the Enigma code.

ANCIENT CIVILIZATIONS

◆ Long before Columbus and the Europeans arrived in the Americas, the largest city outside of central America was the native Mississippians' city of Cahokia, near modern-day St. Louis in the south of Illinois. An astonishingly large and cosmopolitan city for the time—at the center of which was the largest manmade earthen mound in North America—the fate of Cahokia remains unknown. From a peak of perhaps as many as 20,000 people in 1050 CE, the city had been all but abandoned by the mid-1300s for reasons that are still a mystery.

◆ The ancient kingdom of Silla endured on the Korean peninsula for almost nine centuries, until 935 CE. Relatively little is known of its culture, and only a handful of graves and artifacts dating from this time have ever been discovered. In 2013, however, a Silla woman's skeleton was found in Korea, from which historians could discern that she likely survived on a chiefly vegetarian diet of starchy foods, such as rice and wheat.

◆ The civilization around the Indus Valley in northern India thrived around 4,500 years ago. Often described as the first urban civilization in history, the people of the Indus lived in vast and impressive cities with surprisingly modern uniform grid-like layouts and equally modern sewerage and drainage systems. Aside from this, frustratingly little is known of the Indus people—including their language, culture, religion, and much of their everyday lives.

◆ Incredibly, the entire Minoan civilization—one of the most advanced and intricate in the ancient history of Europe—endured on the single Greek island of Crete (an island of similar size to Puerto Rico). Their lavish palaces and other buildings stand in ruins on the island today, and they are some of the most impressive examples of ancient architecture in the world. What the Minoans' fate was, however, remains unclear: the entire island was mysteriously abandoned around 1450 BCE.

◆ The ancient rock city of Petra—with its famous Treasury building cut into the bright red sandstone cliffs of modern-day Jordan—was the highlight of the ancient Nabatean civilization, which thrived in the area from the fourth century BCE to the second century CE. Despite being one of the most advanced civilizations of the ancient world, the Nabateans gradually dwindled as the Roman civilization advanced in its place, and eventually the entire culture disappeared almost 2,000 years ago.

WARTIME PROPOSALS THAT NEVER CAME TO PASS

◆ Operational Sea Lion was Nazi Germany's codename for the eventual planned invasion of Allied England. Due to have been the centerpiece of what we now know as the Battle of Britain, Hitler had presumed that after France fell under Nazi rule, Britain would soon capitulate and accept his control. In the end, however, Germany never gained sufficient control of either the northwest coast of mainland Europe, the English Channel, or the strategic airbases and other locations an air and sea invasion of Great Britain would necessitate. And as Britain continued to fight on the continent, and Hitler's war eventually faltered, the operation never came to fruition.

◆ Operation Bernhard was the code name the Nazis gave to a bizarre plan they concocted to flood Great Britain with counterfeit banknotes. SS Major Bernhard Kruger was put in charge of the scheme, which saw around one million fake pounds produced in special printing workshops—manned by prisoners with printing and engraving experience—at the Sachsenhausen concentration camp, near Oranienburg, in eastern Germany. Much of the money never found its way to England, however, and was instead used to pay spies (with one Turkish spy, Elyesa Bazna, even going so far as to sue the German government for fraudulent payments). After the war, the cash was dumped in a lake in Austria and was rediscovered in 1959.

◆ After the fall of France in 1940, Hitler oversaw the organization of Operation Tannanbaum—a mooted Nazi invasion of Switzerland, despite the country remaining neutral. The plans were never put in motion, however, for a variety of reasons— including the geographic difficulty of a northern or eastern assault on the Alpine nation, the heavily armed population (whose level of gun ownership reportedly matched that of the German army), and Switzerland's openness to the Nazi's use of its trains to ferry supplies between Germany and Italy.

◆ In the event that the use of atomic weaponry was not sanctioned, the United States prepared for another end to the Pacific arena of World War II, with the organization of Operation Downfall—a proposed Allied invasion of Japan. Further divided into two separate operations, the proposal was that troops would first aim to capture the southernmost Japanese island of Kyushu (Operation Olympic) on November 1, 1945, while a second operation would involve an assault on Tokyo (Operation Coronet). A combined force of chiefly American and British troops might have ended up numbering up to one million men had the plans ever been instigated, but in the end, the war came to a different conclusion.

◆ As World War II came to an end, the British forces under Churchill were well aware that the Soviet Union's support of the Allies' cause had been uneasy and feared that an eventual clash with Russia seemed inevitable. As a result, the British drew up a series of contingency plans in the event that military action against the Soviet Union were ever to take place, under the code name Operation Unthinkable. Mercifully, the plans were never required and were later shelved by the British government.

THE DYATLOV PASS INCIDENT

O ne of the most bizarre and mysterious tales in modern history took place high on a mountain pass in the Ural Mountains of western Russia in 1951.

Nine experienced Russian cross-country ski hikers—many of them students from the Soviet Union's Ural Polytechnic Institute—set off on a snowbound expedition into the Ural Mountains in late January 1951. Led by student Igor Dyatlov, the plan was to hike 190 miles through mountainous terrain over the next 16 days, eventually arriving in the mountain village of Vizhay, from where they would telegram the institute to confirm their arrival. When no contact came, however, a search party was launched on February 20 to locate the group—at which point it was found that all nine members of the group had perished in extraordinarily bizarre circumstances.

All that is known of what happened to the group comes from a sequence of photographs that were found on one of the group's cameras and the state of the group's final campsite. After six days of trekking, the search party found the first of the group's tents, which had been sliced open. The near-naked bodies of two of the hikers were found a mile from the tent, with three more found a few days later; the final four bodies were found later in the spring, after the worst of the snows had melted.

Examination of the hikers' bodies found that some had experienced crushing chest injuries—while another was gruesomely missing their tongue, eyes, parts of their mouth and face, as well as part of their skull. The state of this body led to a criminal investigation being launched, but it was eventually concluded that all nine deaths were due to a "spontaneous power of nature"—likely a vast slab avalanche, with the mutilated body perhaps the work of scavenging animals—and the case was closed. But the Soviet government promptly made the case classified, and with so much secrecy surrounding what had happened, the true nature of the Dyatlov incident quickly began to arouse suspicion.

Although several theories have been proposed over the years—ranging from alien activity to the top-secret testing of some manner of military weapons or aircraft—what caused the fate of the nine Dyatlov hikers remains a contentious mystery.

ALL ABOARD! PEOPLE WHO MISSED THE *TITANIC*

◆ Nobel-winner and wireless radio inventor Guglielmo Marconi is known for becoming something of a hero in the aftermath of the *Titanic* sinking, as it was his technology that had alerted ships in the area to the disaster and ensured they arrived in time to rescue passengers from the water. Marconi himself, however, had been due to travel on board the *Titanic*, before changing his plans and traveling across the Atlantic just a matter of days earlier on the Lusitania.

◆ New York businessman, notable arts patron, and Carnegie Steel Company chairman Henry Clay Frick and his wife had booked a suite on board the *Titanic* for a return trip from Europe. Frick's wife, however, sprained her ankle just days before they were due to depart, and so the couple decided to remain in Europe a little longer to allow her to recover.

◆ J.C. Penney, the founder of the store that still bears his name, bought a ticket for the *Titanic*'s return voyage from New York back to Europe. The voyage, of course, never took place, and Penney never completed his journey on what would have been the *Titanic*'s second transatlantic trip.

◆ Multimillionaire business heir Alfred Gwynne Vanderbilt, aged 34 years, had been due to travel on the *Titanic* but canceled his trip so late in the day that some newspapers reported that he was indeed on board when the ship sank. In fact, he had remained in Europe a little longer.

◆ The American novelist and journalist Theodore Dreiser had been due to travel back home to the US from Europe on board the *Titanic*, but his publisher convinced him to take a ticket on board a less lavish ship, the *Kroonland*. The 40-year-old was on board the *Kroonland* when news of the *Titanic*'s fate reached him. He later recounted the moment in his memoir, *A Traveler at Forty*, writing of his terror at the idea of "a ship as immense as the *Titanic* ... sinking in endless fathoms of water," with "two thousand passengers, routed like rats from their berths, only to float helplessly in miles of water, praying and crying!"

TOP TEN: BLOODIEST BATTLES

A lthough estimates of the number of casualties caused by wars and battles are notoriously difficult to ascertain—most notably those in antiquity—most historians agree that the Battle of Stalingrad, at the height of World War II, is likely the bloodiest battle in human history.

♦♦ 1 ♦♦
Battle of Stalingrad (1942–43)
4.1 million *estimated casualties*

♦♦ 2 ♦♦
Siege of Leningrad (1941–44)
4 million

♦♦ 3 ♦♦
Siege of Baghdad (1258)
2 million

♦♦ 4 ♦♦
Battle of Berlin (1945)
1.3 million

♦♦ 5 ♦♦
Siege of Gurganj (1221)
1.2 million

♦♦ 6 ♦♦
Battle of Kiev (1941)
760,000

♦♦ 7 ♦♦
1st Battle of Voronezh (1942)
662,000

♦♦ 8 ♦♦
Siege of Osaka (1614–15)
500,000

♦♦ 9 ♦♦
Battle of Manila (1945)
500,000

♦♦ 10 ♦♦
Siege of Carthage (149–146 BCE)
450,000

MUSIC

TOP TEN: BIGGEST-SELLING ALBUMS OF ALL TIME

A lbum sales figures are difficult to judge precisely (especially now that figures include streaming and downloads, as well as physical media), and claimed sales figures are often far higher than the figure that can be ascertained from the actual retail record. Nevertheless, Michael Jackson's *Thriller* is widely said to have remained the best-selling album in the history of popular music, with somewhere in the region of 51 million—but perhaps as many as 70 million—copies sold since its release in 1982.

◆◆ 1 ◆◆
Michael Jackson, *Thriller* (1982)
51.3 million copies (certified)

◆◆ 2 ◆◆
Eagles, *Their Greatest Hits*
1971–1975 (1976) 41.2 million

◆◆ 3 ◆◆
Eagles, *Hotel California* (1976)
31.8 million

◆◆ 4 ◆◆
AC/DC, *Back in Black* (1980)
31.2 million

◆◆ 5 ◆◆
Shania Twain, *Come on Over*
(1997) 30.4 million

◆◆ 6 ◆◆
Fleetwood Mac, *Rumours* (1977)
30 million

◆◆ 7 ◆◆
Whitney Houston, *The Bodyguard*
(Soundtrack) (1992) 28.7 million

◆◆ 8 ◆◆
Pink Floyd, *The Dark Side of the
Moon* (1973) 24.8 million

◆◆ 9 ◆◆
Bee Gees, *Saturday Night Fever*
(1977) 22.1 million

◆◆ 10 ◆◆
Meat Loaf, Bat Out of Hell (1977)
22 million

MISHEARD LYRICS

J imi Hendrix, "Purple Haze": Perhaps one of the most famous examples of a misheard lyric in music history, it's often wrongly claimed that Jimi Hendrix exclaims "Excuse me while I kiss this guy" rather than "kiss the sky" in his classic 1967 hit.

The Police, "Message in a Bottle": The real line here is, "A year has passed since I wrote my note." But some Police fans have nevertheless long assumed Sting is actually singing, "A year has passed since I broke my nose."

Nirvana, "Smells Like Teen Spirit": Confusion between the actual chorus and a previous rhyme with the word "contagious" has apparently led to some people believing Kurt Cobain is singing "Here we are now, in containers." The correct line is, of course, "Here we are now, entertain us."

Bob Dylan, "Blowin' in the Wind": A classic misheard lyric among Dylan fans the world over is the refrain to his breakout 1963 hit. Although we all know the real line is "The answer, my friend, is blowin' in the wind," some have claimed to hear, "These ants are my friends. They're blowin' in the wind."

Lil Nas X and Billy Ray Cyrus, "Old Town Road": As the title of Lil Nas X's debut smash hit would suggest, the correct lyric here is "I'm gonna take my horse to the old town road"—not, as some listeners would have you believe, "I'm gonna take my horse to the watering hole."

Taylor Swift, "Blank Space": No, Taylor Swift didn't sing about "Starbucks lovers" in her 2014 global smash hit. The refrain line in question is, "Got a long list of ex-lovers," but many listeners and fans alike continue to mishear it as, "All the lonely Starbucks lovers."

Elvis Presley, "Suspicious Minds": The "We're caught in a trap" line in "Suspicious Minds" is said, by some fans at least, to morph into "Recordin' a track" after a few listens!

THE WORLD'S FIRST MODERN STADIUM TOUR, 1969

I t was the Beatles who famously brought stadium rock to a mass audience in August 1965, when they played to an at-the-time record crowd of 55,000 screaming fans at Shea Stadium in New York (earning over $300,000 for 28 minutes' work in the process).

Before then, Elvis Presley had taken his place in history as the first artist to complete a tour entirely in stadiums, rather than smaller or more bespoke music venues, when he embarked on a five-date tour of the Pacific Northwest eight years earlier, in August and September 1957.

But in the early days of stadium gigs, few venues were adequately furnished with sound and light equipment to make the concert itself as musically robust and as visually engaging as the crowd in attendance. Reportedly, one of the reasons why the Beatles stopped touring altogether in 1966 was the inability of larger venues to supply the band with an adequate stage and sound system to support their act. All that changed, however, when the Rolling Stones embarked on their first tour of North America in three years in 1969.

Now at the height of their fame, the band was keen to play in arenas, rather than music venues, and as a result invested heavily in both sound equipment and staging. An entirely new amplification system was developed to support the band and ensure that fans throughout the venue would be able to hear them, while the band also enlisted Broadway and music festival staging impresario Chip Monck to oversee the lighting and design of the stage. Behind the scenes, the Stones' managers spent weeks sourcing the best arenas for the band to play in (and securing the best deal for each one). This combination of cutting-edge onstage equipment and backstage preparation made the entire gig a roaring success. The "first mythic rock and roll tour," as legendary critic Robert Christgau later called it, would end up being a landmark in the history of modern music.

PUSHING THE LIMITS: PROGRESSIVE POP AND ROCK TRACKS

◆ Dionne Warwick, "Anyone Who Had a Heart": A hit on both sides of the Atlantic for several different artists over the years (including British singer Cilla Black), Dionne Warwick's "Anyone Who Had a Heart" was written by legendary songwriter Burt Bacharach. It is notable for its use of multiple different time signatures, as although the track is written in a standard 4/4 time overall, it shifts into 5/4 and 7/8 time throughout, making it a challenge for musicians and singers alike. Warwick's "I Say a Little Prayer," also written by Bacharach, similarly shifts from 4/4 into 10/4 and 11/4 for its chorus.

◆ Fleetwood Mac, "Albatross": In the entire history of the Billboard charts, there have only been 25 instrumental chart-toppers, the vast majority of which were in the days of jazz, big bands, and early disco in the 1950s and 60s. In 1968, however, rock band Fleetwood Mac—who had until then been known for hits like "Black Magic Woman" and "Need Your Love So Bad"—released a three-minute chillout instrumental guitar piece called "Albatross." The track was a number one hit in the UK and reached the top four on the US "Bubbling Under" chart, setting the band on the road to superstardom.

◆ Taylor Swift, "All Too Well (Taylor's Version)": Taylor Swift's re-recordings of her first albums led to the longest Number One hit in the history of the Billboard chart: her re-recorded version of "All Too Well," originally recorded for her 2012 album *Red*, ran to ten minutes and 13 seconds. The longest song ever to chart on the Billboard Hot 100 is André 3000's 2023 hit "I Swear, I Really Wanted to Make a Rap Album but This Is Literally the Way the Wind Blew Me This Time," which runs to 12 minutes and 20 seconds.

◆ The Beach Boys, "Good Vibrations": The Beach Boys were well known for their experimental arrangements, with Brian Wilson spearheading many of their most adventurous sounds. Their classic hit "Good Vibrations" was no different, with Wilson opting to add a bizarre electronic instrument called a theremin into the final mix.

◆ Fleetwood Mac, "Gold Dust Woman": Another classic track known for its use of unusual instrumentation (if it can be called that...) is the Stevie Nicks-led Fleetwood Mac hit "Gold Dust Woman." Knowing that the song's climax needed to sound like no other, the band broke sheets of glass and added the sound of the shattering panes into the percussion!

BEHIND THE MUSIC: THE SONGWRITERS OF FAMOUS HITS

◆ Kenny Rogers and Dolly Parton, "Islands in the Stream": The 1983 global smash hit sold three million copies in the US alone and spent two weeks at the top of the Billboard charts. Neither artist was responsible for the track's songwriting, though, as it was actually written by the Bee Gees.

◆ Kelly Clarkson, "Breakaway": The title track and lead single from Kelly Clarkson's 2004 album Breakaway was written by Avril Lavigne and originally intended to be included on her 2002 debut album *Let Go*. Instead, the track was shelved before it was handed over to Clarkson, who originally recorded it for the soundtrack to *The Princess Diaries 2* in 2004.

◆ Tina Turner, "Private Dancer": A 1984 top-ten hit for Tina Turner, the track was in fact written by Dire Straits frontman Mark Knopfler for the UK band's 1982 album *Love Over Gold*. Realizing that the lyrics of the song were better suited to a female vocalist, Knopfler shelved the song before offering it to Turner two years later.

◆ Tina Turner, "GoldenEye": In 1995, Tina Turner had another global hit on her hands with the theme tune to Pierce Brosnan's first James Bond movie, *GoldenEye*. After producers approached Turner to record the next Bond song, they wanted a similarly legendary songwriting team to work on a track for her and asked none other than vocalist Bono and guitarist The Edge from Irish rock band U2.

◆ Rihanna and Calvin Harris, "This Is What You Came For": Co-written by producer Calvin Harris, Rihanna's 2016 hit is also credited to Swedish songwriter Nils Sjöberg—which is a pseudonym of Harris' then-girlfriend, Taylor Swift.

THE REVIEW THAT CHANGED BRUCE SPRINGSTEEN'S LIFE

N ow one of the world's biggest rock stars, Bruce Springsteen's career began back in 1964 when he bought his first guitar at an appliance store in New Jersey. Soon afterwards, he started playing small-scale gigs in local music venues—taking out a loan in order to upgrade his original $18 guitar for a much improved $60 model—and began recording with a local band called the Castiles.

Until the end of the '60s, Springsteen continued to work with several local bands and session groups, including a trio known as Earth and a rock band called Child (later Steel Mill) whose lineup went on to also include future E Street Band members Vinnie Roslin and Steven Van Zandt, among others. As frontman, Springsteen began to amass something of a cult following, and before long, Steel Mill was one of the most talked about bands in New Jersey—which soon brought them to the attention of an acclaimed music critic, Philip Elwood. Little did Springsteen know that Elwood's review of one of the band's shows would alter the entire trajectory of his career.

It was in January 1970 that Springsteen and his fellow Steel Mill members traveled across the country to play at a venue called The Matrix in San Francisco in support of singer-songwriter Boz Scaggs. Elwood was in the audience and was by all accounts astonished by the evening's opening act. "I have never been so overwhelmed by a totally unknown talent," he wrote in the

San Francisco Examiner, seemingly more impressed by Steel Mill than he was by the main act. The band, he wrote, had a "cohesive musicality" unlike any other he had seen, while lead songwriter and frontman Springsteen was clearly "a most impressive composer."

Elwood's review understandably caused a stir on the California music scene. Within a matter of days, Springsteen and the band had been offered a $1,000 recording contract. Surprisingly, they turned the offer down and returned home to New Jersey, where they continued to hone their act. Eventually, the name Steel Mill was ditched, the E Street Band moniker was chosen instead, and a year later, they signed an even more lucrative contract with Columbia Records.

And the rest, as they say, is music history.

AMAZING INSTRUMENTS

◆ Also known as a bowl organ or hydrocrystalophone, the glass harmonica is a bizarre musical instrument invented by none other than Benjamin Franklin in 1761. The instrument consists of a revolving series of tuned glass disks, or bowls, which—like running a finger around the rim of a wine glass—produce a high-pitched tone when a player's dampened finger is held against them as they turn. The harmonica was a voguish instrument in the late 1700s and early 1800s, with composers such as Mozart, Beethoven, and Strauss all writing pieces and parts for it in their compositions. Even Marie Antoinette is said to have taken lessons on it as a child!

◆ When it came to soundtracking the Vikings' heavenly kingdom of Valhalla in his epic Ring Cycle of operas, German composer Richard Wagner knew he needed an instrument that sounded unlike anything else. His solution was quite simply to invent his own, with the help of noted instrument-maker (and inventor of the saxophone) Adolphe Sax. The so-called Wagner tuba—resembling a cross between a traditional tuba and a French horn and sounding like a French horn crossed with a trombone—was the result, and its striking sound can be heard in several of his compositions.

◆ Invented in 1967, the stylophone is a miniature electronic analog keyboard that produces a whining theremin-like tone. Unlike other keyboard instruments, however, the keys of a stylophone are played with a stylus attached by a cord to the body of the instrument itself, while the keys are flat, allowing the stylus to be run smoothly over all of them to produce a single continuous rising or falling tone.

◆ Inspired by the cubist artworks of Pablo Picasso himself, the Pikasso is a 42-string guitar, fitted with four necks and two sound holes, with networks of strings crossing over each one and across one another. The brainchild of Canadian folksinger and luthier (i.e., guitar-maker) Linda Manzer, the Pikasso was made specifically for jazz musician Pat Metheny in 1984.

◆ The serpent is the striking name given to a bizarrely sinuous wind instrument invented in the late 1500s, which produces a hollow and smooth sound somewhere between a euphonium and a bassoon. Featuring six tone holes and a trombone's mouthpiece and coated in dark black leather, the instrument is unlike any other in the brass or woodwind family.

WHY WE WRITE MUSIC
THE WAY WE DO

J ust like learning to read and write, our ability to write down music allows tunes to be learned and circulated, sung and performed in groups, and passed on from one generation to the next. But as any musician will tell you, musical notation can be extraordinarily complex, with different combinations of pitching clefs, note lengths, accents, sharps, flats, accidentals, bars, and musical measures all required to record a composition on paper accurately. So, how did we develop such a complex—yet utterly perfect—system of writing music?

The origins of musical notation go back to the days of Ancient Greece, when the mathematician Pythagoras (perhaps better known for his work on right triangles) noticed that harmonic intervals between musical notes relied on arithmetical ratios, demonstrating his discovery on the lengths of musical strings being tightened to different levels of tension. This mathematical understanding of music set in place many of the fundamental elements that continue to underpin musical compositions today, including scales, tunings, and harmonies.

For the next thousand years or so, however, there was no way of passing on an understanding of music accurately without seeing or hearing a demonstration of it and learning a melody by ear or by memory. By the medieval era, however, music had become increasingly important in European religion, with plainsong and so-called Gregorian chants (named after music-loving

Pope Gregory I) becoming popular in the 800s CE. Circulating this religious music continent-wide ultimately necessitated the development of a means of writing music down, so that hymns and chants in praise of God could be enjoyed as widely as possible.

It was in the early 1000s that an Italian Benedictine monk and music instructor named Guido D'Arezzo began developing a system to do precisely that. It was he who introduced the idea of the musical stave, or staff, consisting of a series of lines (and the spaces between them) representing the different notes of a scale. He also devised time signatures and a sequence of marks representing different notes—but as ingenious as D'Arezzo's system was, he had no way of showing how long each note should sound.

That final development was the brainchild of a German-born musician named Franco of Cologne, who, in the mid-1200s, introduced a set of symbols, each representing a different note length. A century later, Franco's system was greatly improved and expanded by another European musical figure named Philippe de Vitry, whose contributions formed the groundwork of the minims, breves, and crotchets that we still use today.

TOP TEN:
BIGGEST-SELLING ARTISTS

◆◆ 1 ◆◆

The Beatles
600 million estimated
record sales

◆◆ 2 ◆◆

Elvis Presley
500 million

◆◆ 3 ◆◆

Michael Jackson
450 million

◆◆ 4 ◆◆

Elton John
300 million

◆◆ 5 ◆◆

Queen
300 million

◆◆ 6 ◆◆

Madonna
300 million

◆◆ 7 ◆◆

Led Zeppelin
250 million

◆◆ 8 ◆◆

Rihanna
250 million

◆◆ 9 ◆◆

Eminem
220 million

◆◆ 10 ◆◆

Pink Floyd
200 million

BOREDOM BUSTERS 3

What has 88 keys but usually only one lock?

◆◆

Only one odd number becomes even when you take away one-fifth of it.

What number is it?

◆◆

How many months have 28 days?

◆◆

What slows you down when you open it?

◆◆

What has hands and a face but cannot clap or see?

(Find solutions on page 196.)

GEOGRAPHY

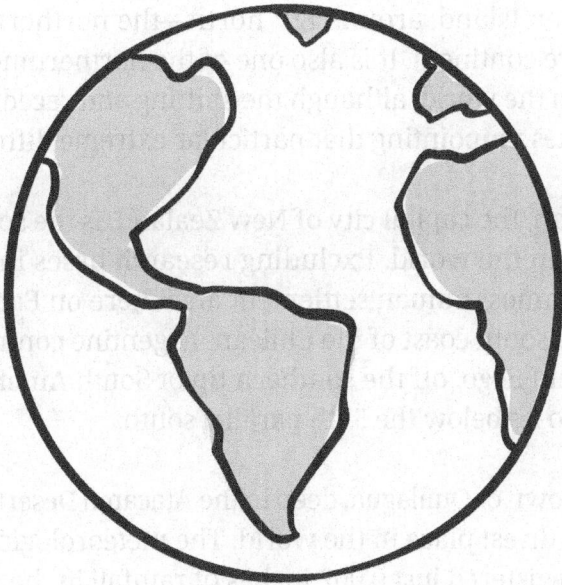

EARTH'S EXTREMES

◆ The deepest point on the surface of the Earth is the Challenger Deep—part of the larger Mariana Trench in the western Pacific Ocean—which drops to a maximum depth of 35,814 feet below sea level. Fewer people have explored the very deepest part of the ocean than have set foot on the surface of the moon.

◆ Although Greenland is politically part of Denmark, geographically it lies in North America, making its northernmost point—Kaffeklubben Island, around 80° north—the northernmost point on the entire continent. It is also one of the northernmost points of solid land in the world, although the shifting and receding of Arctic Sea ice makes pinpointing that particular extreme difficult.

◆ Wellington, the capital city of New Zealand, is the southernmost capital city in the world. Excluding research bases in Antarctica, the southernmost human settlement anywhere on Earth is Puerto Toro, on the south coast of the Chilean–Argentine controlled island of Tierra del Fuego, off the southern tip of South America. It is the only town to lie below the 55th parallel south.

◆ The tiny town of Quillagua, deep in the Atacama Desert in northern Chile, is the driest place in the world. The meteorological station in Quillagua registered just 0.002 inches of rainfall in the period from 1964 to 2001!

◆ The average wind speed in Commonwealth Bay, Antarctica, is 50 mph, making this inlet on the coast of Antarctica the windiest place in the world. Although strong gusts are recorded here almost continually, speeds of over 150 mph are commonplace.

HOW LONG HAVE WE KNOWN THE WORLD IS ROUND?

I t's a tale we all hear many times in childhood: before Christopher Columbus set sail from Europe to the Americas in 1492, everyone believed the Earth was flat and that he would eventually sail off the edge and out into space.

It's a fun story, certainly—but in truth, people have known that the world is spherical for far, far longer than that tale would have you think.

In fact, the idea that the world is round has endured since the time of the Ancient Greeks. Around 2,500 years ago, various philosophers and mathematicians such as Pythagoras theorized that the Earth was round, in part based on purely aesthetic opinions (i.e., a sphere is a more pleasing shape than any flat plane), and later, on more tangible evidence: because the moon appeared round, due to the ever-changing appearance of its "terminator" (the line between the lit and unlit part of its surface), many early thinkers concluded that it made sense that the Earth was round as well.

Not long after that, another Greek philosopher named Anaxagoras rightly deduced the workings of solar and lunar eclipses, providing yet more weight to the theory of a round Earth. And in 350 BCE, even Aristotle got in on the act by declaring that the Earth was a sphere, based on his observations of the appearance of constellations above the horizon.

Outside of the enlightened world of Ancient Greece, however, many people in the rest of Europe misguidedly continued to believe in a flat Earth right through to the medieval period. As the works of the Greek philosophers became more widely known, however, the notion of a spherical Earth began to spread (although for many centuries longer, this spherical Earth, not the sun, was nevertheless wrongly considered to lie at the center of our solar system).

Ultimately, although the idea of heliocentrism (that the sun lies at the center of our solar system) remained controversial until the Renaissance, the idea of a round Earth was by no means an unusual or contentious one—even by Christopher Columbus' day!

STRANGE PLACE NAMES

- Agency, Iowa, US
- Asbestos, Canada
- Boring, Oregon, US
- Coffin Top, South Georgia
- Dildo, Canada
- Fortification, New Zealand
- Hazard, Kentucky, US
- Lit, Sweden
- Mad, Slovakia
- Mousehole, UK
- Police, Poland
- Rust, Austria
- Sense, Switzerland
- Toast, North Carolina, US

- Alert, North Carolina, US
- Batman, Turkey
- Catbrain, UK
- Die, France
- Fail, Portugal
- Germ, France
- Intercourse, Pennsylvania, US
- Love, Oklahoma, US
- Mayo, Ireland
- Nose, Japan
- Rimsting, Germany
- Sandwich, UK
- Shop, UK
- Wealthy, Texas, US

WHO PRODUCED THE FIRST MAP OF THE WORLD?

T hese days, you can find maps of the world everywhere, from apps on your phone to the artwork on banknotes. But historically, so lacking was our knowledge of the true extent of our world that many early maps had no notion of just how vast the Earth was, not to mention how our nations, islands, and continents are laid out upon it.

Many early maps of the world were, ultimately, fairly limited. In the sixth century BCE, for instance, a Greek philosopher and geographer named Anaximander produced one of the most extensive and detailed maps of the world of the time. Yet, it was limited to what was known of Europe, Asia, and North Africa (which he labeled Libya) at the time, around which he believed was a single circulating ocean, with no hint yet of the existence of the Americas, Australia, and the poles. So, who produced the very first complete world map?

Understandably, much of our knowledge of the world had to wait until the Age of Exploration, when places like Australia and Antarctica were finally explored by Westerners who could then plot them onto their maps of the world. Even long after these places were first visited by Westerners, however, much of their geography remained unknown: a world map produced in the mid-1600s by a legendary Dutch cartographer named Joan Bleau—known as the Nova et accuratissima totius terrarum orbis tabula, or "New and Very Accurate Map of the Whole World"—included both the Americas and Australia, but not their most extreme coasts, as they had still not yet been mapped.

In fact, it was not until the 18th and 19th centuries that our notion of the layout of the world as we know it today finally began to take shape. With the far northern stretches of Arctic Canada and Siberia now explored, and Australia mapped and circumnavigated for the first time in 1803, Colton's map-making company in New York produced a world map by artist and engraver D. Griffing Johnson in 1831 that included all but the very furthest corners of the world.

ALMOST A COUNTRY: NATIONS ONLY PARTIALLY RECOGNIZED

◆ At just over 3,300 square miles in size (roughly the size of two Rhode Islands), the tiny Republic of Abkhazia declared independence from the former Soviet nation of Georgia in 1999. Located on Georgia's northern border with Russia, nestled on the Black Sea, Abkhazia has existed in some form or another for centuries, and at one point was a major component state of the Byzantine Empire. As of the 21st century, however, despite declaring its independence, it remains only partially recognized on an international level, with only a handful of UN member nations considering it an independent state.

◆ Known to many western nations as Western Sahara, the Sahrawi Arab Democratic Republic, or SADR, is a vast state on the Atlantic coast of northwest Africa. Once a colony of Spain, the territory's northern neighbor, Morocco, invaded and annexed the territory in 1975 and has continued to defend its claim to the SADR ever since—a claim supported by the United States but contested by more than 40 fellow UN member states. The true status of the territory remains controversial, despite several geopolitical attempts to resolve the situation.

◆ A tiny, landlocked sliver of 1,600 square miles of territory along the border between Ukraine and Moldova, Transnistria (known locally as Pridnestrovie) declared its independence in 1990 amidst the breakup of the Soviet Union. Internationally, however, most nations continue to see the breakaway state as part of Moldovan territory and, after a resolution ending a brief period of fighting in Transnistria in the early 1990s, it has maintained that standing for over 30 years. The state has its own constitution, flag, coat of arms, national anthem, postal service, and several other separate institutions, but today it remains a hangover from the Soviet breakup, and its future remains unresolved.

◆ The northern stretch of the East African Republic of Somalia is known as Somaliland, and it claims independence as a partially recognized nation in its own right. The nation's roots lie in two former European colonies, Italian and British Somaliland, which were united as an independent nation, the Somali Republic, in 1960. Since then, however, the old borders of the past have remained controversial, and Somaliland—the successor state to British Somaliland—has fought hard to be considered an independent nation.

HOW DO WE KNOW
WHAT LATITUDE AND
LONGITUDE ARE?

T oday, you pick up a map and see lines of latitude and longitude clearly marked on it. From there, you can deduce the relative location of different places around the world. Lines of latitude are regularly spaced parallels relative to the equator, while lines of longitude stretch from north to south on the globe, perpendicular to latitude.

The notion of dividing up maps of the world using grid lines like these dates back to the third century BCE, when a geographer and astronomer named Eratosthenes began using networks of lines to irregularly divide his maps of the world and the heavens as they were known at the time. His work formed the basis of all similar systems of latitude and longitude since.

Around 500 years later, the Egyptian scholar Ptolemy built on Eratosthenes' work by dividing the world (as it was known to the Romans at the time) using a series of lines based around the equator for latitude and the so-called Fortunate Islands (now the Canary Islands) for longitude. He included this early chart of Europe and North Africa in his seminal *Geographia*, which, much like Eratosthenes' method before it, formed a new groundwork for all future cartographic work.

By the Middle Ages, a similar system of so-called rhumb lines had come into operation, using magnetic north as its focus. Complex maps and navigational charts known as "portolan" charts were produced that were crisscrossed with often vast networks of these rhumb lines, or loxodromes, which worked as paths of constant bearing relative to magnetic north. The curvature of the Earth meant that these charts were only accurate over relatively short distances, however—and so, as vessels capable of global travel became increasingly commonplace, a new approach that worked worldwide was necessary.

At long last, in 1569, a Flemish mapmaker named Gerardus Mercator produced a map of the world that straightened these rhumb lines out. This had the unavoidable effect of slightly morphing the appearance of the continents in the process. However, this slight rearrangement of the appearance of the world was a small price to pay given what Mercator's projection had achieved: any straight line drawn on a Mercator map was, like the parallel and perpendicular lines that crossed it, a line of constant bearing, allowing navigators to easily plot and follow a perfectly straight course.

TOP TEN:
BIGGEST COUNTRIES

◆◆ 1 ◆◆
Russia
(6,601,667 mi2)

◆◆ 2 ◆◆
Canada
(3,855,100 mi2)

◆◆ 3 ◆◆
China
(3,705,410 mi2)

◆◆ 4 ◆◆
United States
(3,677,647 mi2)

◆◆ 5 ◆◆
Brazil
(3,285,862 mi2)

◆◆ 6 ◆◆
Australia
(2,988,900 mi2)

◆◆ 7 ◆◆
India
(1,269,219 mi2)

◆◆ 8 ◆◆
Argentina
(1,073,500 mi2)

◆◆ 9 ◆◆
Kazakhstan
(1,052,090 mi2)

◆◆ 10 ◆◆
Algeria
(919,595 mi2)

TOP TEN:
SMALLEST COUNTRIES

◆◆ 1 ◆◆

Vatican City
(0.19 mi2)

◆◆ 2 ◆◆

Monaco
(0.77 mi2)

◆◆ 3 ◆◆

Nauru
(8.1 mi2)

◆◆ 4 ◆◆

Tuvalu
(10 mi2)

◆◆ 5 ◆◆

San Marino
(24 mi2)

◆◆ 6 ◆◆

Liechtenstein
(62 mi2)

◆◆ 7 ◆◆

Marshall Islands
(70 mi2)

◆◆ 8 ◆◆

Saint Kitts and Nevis
(101 mi2)

◆◆ 9 ◆◆

Maldives
(115 mi2)

◆◆ 10 ◆◆

Malta
(122 mi2)

BOREDOM BUSTERS 4

Forwards, I am very heavy. Backwards, I am not. What am I?

◆ ◆

Donald's father had three sons. Huey and Dewey were two of them—what was the name of the third?

◆ ◆

The more of them you take, the more of them you leave behind. What are they?

◆ ◆

I am a powder, the process of removing powder, and the process of applying powder. What am I?

◆ ◆

My blanket is so big, it could cover the entire town. What is it made from?

(Find solutions on page 196.)

SPORTS & GAMES

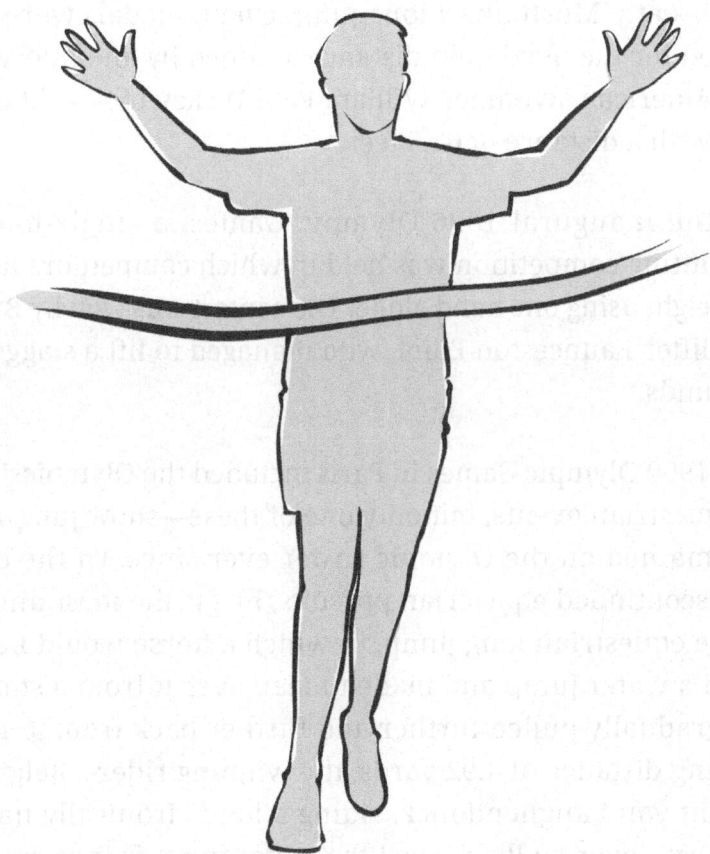

FORMER OLYMPIC SPORTS

◆ At the 1904 Olympic Games in St. Louis, the swimming roster of events included a competition for plunge diving. Competitors would dive into a pool from a standing start and then continue to drift through the water for up to 60 seconds, or until they ran out of breath. Much like a long jump event, medals were then awarded for the maximum distance attained by an underwater diver. American swimmer William Paul Dickey took gold in the event, with a distance of 62.5 feet.

◆ At the inaugural 1896 Olympic Games, a single-handed weightlifting competition was held in which competitors had to lift a weight using one hand alone. The contest was won by British weightlifter Launceston Elliot, who managed to lift a staggering 156 pounds.

◆ The 1900 Olympic Games in Paris included the Olympics' very first equestrian events, but only one of these—show jumping—has remained on the Olympic roster ever since. Of the other four discontinued equestrian pursuits, by far the most unusual was the equestrian long jump, in which a horse would be run toward a water jump and made to leap over it from a starting point gradually pulled further and further back from it. From a starting distance of 4.92 yards, the winning rider—Belgium's Constant van Langhendonck, riding a horse ironically named Extra-Dry—eventually cleared the water jump from a starting position of 7.54 yards.

◆ Several team and field sports have been abandoned over the years at the Olympics, with pelota, cricket, croquet, rugby, and jeu de paume (also known as real or court tennis) all featured in the early days of the Games.

◆ Golf was featured in the Olympic Games just twice in its very earliest days. In 1900, there were both male and female golfing competitions, while in 1904, the women's game was swapped out for a special team competition before the sport was dropped from the Olympic roster the following year. After a 116-year hiatus, however, golf was brought back as an Olympic event for the Rio Games in 2016, and it has remained an Olympic sport ever since.

THE ORIGINAL MARATHON

I t's one of the most famous stories in sporting history: after the legendary Battle of Marathon in 490 BCE, a soldier named Pheidippides ran a distance of 26 miles back to Athens to bring news of the Greek victory over the Persians.

The accuracy of that tale has been debated for centuries, with the name now attached to it, Pheidippides, largely thought to have been conflated with that of another soldier who ran a similarly large distance from Athens to Sparta. But not only is the true origin of the marathon a somewhat sketchy tale, so too is the origin of its length.

A standard marathon—run at venues all around the world, as well as the Summer Olympic Games—is now measured at precisely 26 miles and 385 yards. But that was neither the distance said to have been run by Pheidippides, nor has that always been the standard. In fact, early Olympic marathons were run over a non-standard distance, judged merely to be somewhere in the region of the mid-20-mile mark. At the very first revived Olympics in 1896, for instance, the marathon course was actually closer to 25 miles, as it was in 1900. At the 1904 St. Louis games, the marathon was run over 24 miles and 1,500 yards, and the distance continued to change over the next two decades.

The marathon distance as it is today, in fact, was not standardized until the 1924 Olympic Games in Paris—when the decision was made to mirror that of the British Olympic Committee, who had in turn adopted a standard of 26 miles, 385 yards, for the 1908 Games in London. Back then, that distance had been arranged purely by chance as the organizers wished to have the marathon begin at Windsor Castle and end in front of the royal box at London's Wembley Stadium. In the aftermath of the 1908 race, the British adopted this royal distance as their standard, and the world simply followed suit in the 1920s.

THE FOUR-MINUTE MILE STORY

Another athletic milestone is that of the four-minute mile, an extraordinary feat that was achieved back in 1954 by the British runner Roger Bannister.

Before then, running a mile in under four minutes had long been considered an athletic step too far, but as training techniques and athletic endurance gradually improved over the decades, runner after runner came tantalizingly close to achieving it. At long last, on a blustery day in May in Oxford, UK, Bannister completed the unthinkable in a time of 3 minutes, 59.4 seconds—a full two seconds faster than any previous attempt.

What made Bannister's achievement all the more remarkable was that, as well as being a runner, he was a medical doctor. As such, all his life he had read paper after paper and theory after theory claiming that not only was a sub-four-minute mile likely impossible, but it appeared so unlikely a milestone that anyone even attempting to run that fast for that long would likely die in the process. So not only did Bannister break a record, but he also disproved years of his own profession's theories in the process!

After that first record was broken, however, the floodgates were open. Incredibly, Bannister's four-minute mile time—which broke a 40-year deadlock of attempts at the time—only stood for a matter of weeks, as Australian runner John Landy ran a mile in a time of 3 minutes, 58 seconds on June 21, just 46 days after Bannister.

◆◆

From there, successive athletes continued to improve the record, with New Zealand's John Walker breaking the 3.50 mark in 1975 (with a time of 3 minutes and 49.4 seconds), and Algeria's Noureddine Morceli breaking the 3.45 mark by just .61 seconds in 1993. To date, the current men's mile record is 3 minutes, 43.13 seconds, which was run by Moroccan athlete Hicham El Guerrouj in Rome in 1999.

◆◆

SPORTING INVENTORS

◆ Before the 1960s, high jump competitions typically saw jumpers leap over the bar almost like a racehorse, one leg in front of the other, following a diagonal approach in a curious technique known as a "scissor." All that changed at the 1968 Mexico City Olympics, however, when American athlete Dick Fosbury stunned the world with his own unique jumping style that saw him vault backwards over the bar, leading with the "wrong" foot, in a technique that became known as the "Fosbury flop." By the following Olympics in 1972, Fosbury's technique was already being used by a majority of high jump competitors and has since gone on to become the standard means of leaping the bar.

◆ Outside of his native Mexico, soccer player (turned statesman) Cuauhtémoc Blanco is best known for a move known as the cuauhtemiña: with two opposing players attempting to take the ball from him, Blanco would momentarily trap the ball between his feet and jump through the two attacking players to escape.

◆ The rules of boxing are famously known as the Queensbury rules, in honor of a British nobleman of the Victorian era, John Douglas, the 9th Marquess of Queensbury. The rules themselves—which replaced the so-called London Prize rules of the days of bare-knuckle boxing—were in fact drawn up by a Welsh sportsman named John Graham Chambers. Queensbury merely advocated for their use, and ultimately it was his name that became attached to the code when it was finally published in the press in 1867.

◆ In figure skating, a twisting jump on the ice is famously known as an Axel jump. Contrary to anyone who believes this name refers to the turning "axle" of a motor car, however, this style of jump is actually named after its inventor: the legendary Norwegian figure skater Axel Paulsen. The Lutz jump (Alois Lutz), Salchow (Ulrich Salchow), and Kerrigan spiral (Nancy Kerrigan) are all likewise named after noted skaters.

◆ At the 2002 Winter Olympics, Australian speed skater Steven Bradbury took gold in the 1,000m race after all his competitors crashed out in the final lap. "Bradburying," or "Doing a Bradbury," has since come to be used in Australian sporting terminology to mean winning by default, or as the last person standing, after the removal or disqualification of all opposition.

THE FIRST OLYMPICS

When a movement began to revive the Olympic Games of Ancient Greece as an international competition in the modern era, it made sense that the inaugural modern Games should be held back where they had begun in Athens. But the 1896 Olympics were considerably different from the Games as they are today, in a number of different ways.

For one thing, the first modern Olympics only attracted competitors from 14 different countries—namely Australia, Austria, Bulgaria, Chile, Denmark, France, Germany, Great Britain, Greece, Hungary, Italy, Sweden, Switzerland, and the United States. Greece had a total of 169 competing athletes; Chile sent just one, the 13-year-old sprinter Luis Subercaseaux.

The roster of events was considerably different, too, with a number of modern events missing from the schedule and several bizarre former disciplines included in their place. The 1896 Games, for instance, included a 12-hour cycling race, a military rifle shooting event, a team performance on the gymnastic parallel bars, and a 100m swimming race only open to members of the Greek navy.

The medals, too, were different at the first Olympics, with winners given silver, not gold, and competitors in second place awarded a medal of solid copper. The winning trio of gold, silver, and bronze medals was not introduced until much later, although the International Olympic Committee has since retrospectively awarded first, second, and third place commendations to all the original Olympians.

SPORTING TERMINOLOGY QUIZ

Listed on the left here are ten sporting terms—and jumbled together on the right are the sports in which they would be heard. Match the pairs together.

A Age-uke

B Armstand

C Blunt point

D Conversion

E Counter-parry

F Goaltending

G Googly

H Nassau

I Tablesetter

J Yard sale

1 Archery

2 Baseball

3 Basketball

4 Cricket

5 Diving

6 Fencing

7 Golf

8 Karate

9 Rugby

10 Snowboarding

(Find solutions on page 197.)

PICK A CARD: AMAZING CARD GAME FACTS

◆ Playing cards are among the oldest known items of gaming equipment in human history, with decks as we know them today believed to have originated in China more than 1,200 years ago.

◆ A deck of cards has some unusual parallels to a calendar year, and it has been theorized that the number of suits, cards, and court cards in a standard deck might have once been intended to mirror the coming and going of the year. The four suits, for instance, match the four seasons; the 13 cards in each one matches the 13 lunar cycles of a year and 13 weeks in a quarter; the 12 court cards (four sets of king, queen, jack) in a deck match the 12 months; and the 52 cards overall matches the 52 weeks of the year. Adding up the numerical value of all the cards in a deck, excluding the joker, comes to 364; including the joker brings the total to 365!

◆ Historically, the four suits in a pack of cards weren't always spades, hearts, clubs, and diamonds. Sometimes, one or more of these would be swapped out for items such as swords, gold, coins, and cups, perhaps as gambling and gaming decks became confused with spiritualists' tarot cards.

◆ In mathematical terms, there are 52! (52 factorial) different ways of ordering a deck of cards—a number equivalent to an eight followed by 67 zeroes. It is a number so extraordinarily vast, in fact, that if you were to shuffle a deck of cards, it is statistically unlikely that the resulting order has ever been used in history.

◆ The kings and queens included in a pack of cards were originally modeled on genuine historical figures, and early decks often included caricatures of the likes of Constantine the Great, King Solomon, Henry IV, Julius Caesar, Alexander the Great, and Charlemagne. Over time, the likenesses on the cards became more stylized, however, and the image styles typically used today likely emerged as a series of woodcut prints in medieval France.

TOP TEN: OLYMPIANS

◆◆ 1 ◆◆

Michael Phelps
(US, swimming)
Gold: 23/Silver: 3/
Bronze: 2 = Total 28

◆◆ 2 ◆◆

Larisa Latynina
(USSR, gymnastics)
9/5/4 = 18

◆◆ 3 ◆◆

Marit Bjørgen
(Norway, cross-country skiing)
8/4/3 = 15

◆◆ 4 ◆◆

Nikolay Andrianov
(USSR, gymnastics)
7/5/3 = 15

◆◆ 5 ◆◆

Katie Ledecky
(US, swimming)
9/4/1 = 14

◆◆ 6 ◆◆

Ole Einar Bjørndalen
(Norway, biathlon/cross-
country skiing) 8/4/1 = 13

◆◆ 7 ◆◆

Boris Shakhlin
(USSR, gymnastics)
7/4/2 = 13

◆◆ 8 ◆◆

Ireen Wüst
(Netherlands, speed skating)
6/5/2 = 13

◆◆ 9 ◆◆

Edoardo Mangiarotti
(Italy, fencing)
6/5/2 = 13

◆◆ 10 ◆◆

Ono Takashi (Japan,
gymnastics)
5/4/4 = 13

BOREDOM BUSTERS 5

What has a long neck and rounded shoulders, but no head and no arms?

◆◆

What contains 26 letters, but only three syllables?

◆◆

What becomes more useful as soon as it's broken?

◆◆

What is full of holes but still holds water?

◆◆

I know someone who has married dozens of people—but has never themselves been wed. Who are they?

(Find solutions on page 197.)

NATURE

NATURE'S DEADLIEST ANIMALS

◆ There are three species of taipan snake native to Australia, of which the inland taipan or fierce snake is by far the deadliest. In fact, the venom of a single inland taipan would be potent enough to kill as many as 100 human beings, making it the most venomous terrestrial snake on the planet.

◆ The king cobra is the longest venomous snake in the world, with individuals typically growing to more than eight feet in length. The fastest venomous snake is the African black mamba (also the deadliest snake in Africa), which can move at speeds of over 12 mph.

◆ Although not the most venomous snake in the world, the saw-scaled viper of Africa, the Middle East, and southern Asia is believed to be responsible for more deaths than any other venomous snake in the world. Known for its irritability and tendency to bite when surprised or cornered, the snake kills an estimated 5,000 people every year—equivalent to around one in every 25 snake-related deaths worldwide.

◆ There are more than 2,000 species of scorpion in the world, of which barely 1% carry venom potent enough to kill a human being. Nonetheless, the creatures are so commonplace in the deserts and jungles of the world that around 3,300 people die from scorpion stings every year—with the so-called deathstalker scorpion among the most dangerous.

◆ Sharks might make people afraid to go in the water, but annually, there are fewer than a hundred recorded shark attacks every year, of which fewer than half are considered unprovoked—and, according to 2024's figures, only four were fatal. That makes sharks far less dangerous statistically than lions (which kill around 100 people every year), crocodiles (around 1,000 fatalities), and even elephants (600) and hippos (500). In fact, going by numbers alone, sharks are almost 15,000 times less dangerous than domestic dogs, who are responsible for an average of 59,000 deaths every year.

◆ Oddly, of all the world's deadliest animals, the mosquito is responsible for more deaths per year than any other creature, with around two-thirds of a million malarial fatalities every year. Incredibly, the mosquito is so deadly, in fact, that it is popularly said to be responsible for the deaths of half the human population that has ever lived!

HOW A FINCH GAVE US THE THEORY OF EVOLUTION

It was a theory that changed everything we thought we knew about the world, and it put us on a new trajectory to understanding our place on our planet. So, how did Charles Darwin come up with his theory of evolution?

Darwin was an acclaimed naturalist, of course, who dedicated his life to the study of living things. His writings are full of observations, based on all manner of different creatures, that influenced his thinking. One of the most important creatures in his work, however, was a group of finches that live on the isolated Galapagos Islands in the eastern Pacific Ocean.

Darwin visited the Galapagos Islands for five weeks in the 1830s, during which time he noticed the islands were populated by around a dozen small finch-like birds, which he presumed were the same as the finches and mockingbirds he had seen on the mainland. Having brought several of the birds back home to England with him, however, Darwin consulted an ornithologist named John Gould, who noted that all 12 of the birds Darwin had brought back with him were not finches at all but a distinct family of an entirely different kind of bird called a tanager.

What set these birds apart from their mainland cousins, Gould and Darwin noted, was their beaks, which appeared to be extraordinarily well suited to the different diets and habitats found across the islands. Those that lived on islands, where they mostly fed on seeds, for instance, had tough, wedge-shaped bills useful in cracking the seeds open. Those that mostly fed on insects, meanwhile, had sharper, narrower bills. Lastly, one of the birds that had been observed feeding on blood had an immensely sharp and powerful beak, which it could use to cut the skin of the other creatures on which it fed.

The remarkable diversity and well-suitedness of the birds' beaks set Darwin's thoughts in motion. Eventually, he would theorize that the birds were indeed descended from mainland birds, but in their isolation on the islands had gradually evolved distinct beaks that allowed them to make the most of their new environment and available diet, whatever they may be.

AMAZING ANIMAL ADAPTATIONS

◆ One of the most distinctive animal adaptations in nature is the giraffe's neck, which has become increasingly elongated over evolutionary time to allow the animals to feed at the tops of trees, where other creatures cannot reach. Despite its length, however, the giraffe's neck contains just seven vertebrae—the same number of bones as there are in a human neck.

◆ Whereas some species of sharks, like dogfish, lay eggs, others give birth to live young. And of those that have live young, some act as diligent parents, while others leave their young to fend for themselves. The great white shark falls into the latter category, as these giant creatures remain in their mothers' wombs for more than year, gradually developing in size. Already three feet long by the time they are born, the young shark pups are so well developed that they require no further development, leaving their mother to resume her ordinary life as they head off on their own instantly.

◆ Despite being nonvenomous themselves, North American king snakes have evolved an enzyme in their bodies that breaks down the venom of other snakes, including rattlesnakes and cottonmouths, making them immune to their bites. As a result, king snakes are one of the very few snakes in the world that can feed on venomous snakes, which they kill by constriction. Incredibly, king snakes can eat snakes that are more than a third larger than themselves!

◆ Camels are obviously well suited to desert climates, with even their famous hump consisting of a store of fat to keep the animals nourished when food and water are rare. Besides wide-splaying feet that prevent them from sinking into the sand—and a strategic covering of fur that is thicker in sun-facing areas—one of the camels' most unusual adaptations is a bizarre third eyelid, which helps protect their delicate eyes from wind and sandstorms.

◆ Dorcas gazelles are another desert-dweller who have adopted an extraordinary method of conserving water. Incredibly, they are capable of going many weeks without drinking, and they extract all the water they need from the plants they feed on. Before urinating, however, the gazelles' bodies can also remove all the water that might otherwise be lost in their urine—so instead of producing waste urine, they go to the bathroom by depositing solid lumps of uric acid.

TOP TEN: HEAVIEST TERRESTRIAL CREATURES

All the heaviest creatures in the world are whales, with the blue whale widely held to be the heaviest animal ever to have lived in the history of our planet. This list limits the heaviest animals to terrestrial creatures.

◆◆ **1** ◆◆
African bush elephant
(13,227 lbs average mass)

◆◆ **2** ◆◆
Asian elephant
(9,920 lbs)

◆◆ **3** ◆◆
African forest elephant
(5,952 lbs)

◆◆ **4** ◆◆
White rhinoceros
(4,409 lbs)

◆◆ **5** ◆◆
Indian rhinoceros
(4,188 lbs)

◆◆ **6** ◆◆
Hippopotamus
(3,968 lbs)

◆◆ **7** ◆◆
Javan rhinoceros
(3,858 lbs)

◆◆ **8** ◆◆
Black rhinoceros
(2,425 lbs)

◆◆ **9** ◆◆
Giraffe
(2,204 lbs)

◆◆ **10** ◆◆
Gaur
(2,094 lbs)

HOW THE CEOLACANTH CAME BACK FROM THE DEAD

F rom the dodo to the Tasmanian tiger, tales of animals going extinct are all too common (and flick ahead a few pages for some tales of precisely that).

Every so often, however, a creature long believed to have been lost comes back, seemingly from the dead—which is what happened to a bizarre fish called a coelacanth almost a century ago.

It was way back in 1938 that a group of fishermen working off the coast of South Africa hauled up their trawl nets and saw that they had captured a curious-looking fish none of them had seen before. Taking the fish to South Africa's East London Museum, a naturalist examined it and realized that it was a coelacanth—one of a family of fish that had previously been believed to have died out more than 70 million years ago.

The discovery understandably stunned the scientific community, and news of the "living fossil" fish made headlines all around the world. Since then, several more individuals have been caught by fishermen and researchers alike in the Indian Ocean—though it took many years before anyone had a chance to take a look at a second specimen. Incredibly, after that first captured fish in 1938, another coelacanth wasn't caught in the wild again until 1952!

HOW A STORK
SOLVED THE RIDDLE
OF MIGRATION

L ong before we truly understood the extraordinary ability of
some creatures to travel vast distances around the world each
year, scientists and naturalists had some bizarre theories about the
seasonal and annual disappearance of certain species. Some, such
as swallows and martins, for instance, were believed to hibernate
at the bottom of lakes and ponds (a conclusion seemingly based on
the birds' habit of skimming the water's surface to capture flies).
The 17th-century naturalist Charles Morton had another theory,
however: having only ever seen swallows and swifts flying high
in the sky before unceremoniously vanishing at the end of the
summer, he suggested back in 1680 that the birds must surely fly
all the way to the moon in the wintertime!

With little evidence to disprove them, wild suggestions and
theories like these remained common in the scientific community
for many years—until an extraordinary discovery in 1822 turned
them on their head.

The discovery in question was made on the outskirts of the German
coastal village of Klütz, near Hamburg, when a white stork was
seen flying around the local fields with an entire spear pierced
through its body. The 30-inch weapon had apparently entered
the bird's chest and traveled all the way up its neck, with its point
now lodged near its head, sticking out just below its face. Despite
the injury, the bird appeared to be living perfectly well—but

the reaction to the bizarre sight quickly turned to astonishment when the bird was captured and the spear was found to be from central Africa.

The discovery proved without doubt that birds like this do not hibernate or disappear in the wintertime but must travel vast distances to warmer climates. This particular bird, now known as the "Pfeilstorch," or "arrow stork," had presumably narrowly escaped being hunted by tribespeople during its journey through Africa.

In the decades that followed, other examples of the Pfeilstorch were discovered in Europe, and still today the original 1822 specimen—with the spear stuck through its neck—remains on display in the zoological collection of the University of Rostock.

THE LAST OF ITS KIND: TALES OF EXTINCTION

◆ The entire world population of the dodo bird was once found on the tiny Indian Ocean island of Mauritius. Having presumably lived undisturbed in the wild for centuries without any natural predators, when sailors from Europe began arriving on the island in the early 1500s, the birds naturally felt no need to be fearful or suspicious—which unfortunately made the birds all too easy to stalk, capture, and kill. According to reports from sailors at the time, the dodos were so naturally inquisitive and trusting of the sailors who arrived on the island that they would even walk up to the boiling cauldrons of water they had prepared and could be picked up and thrown into the pot without a struggle. The ease of hunting eventually proved too much, however, and the very final dodo bird is believed to have been killed in 1681.

◆ Woolly mammoths stood upwards of 12 feet tall, could weigh up to six tons, and were armed with long, curved, elephant-like tusks that could grow up to 15 feet long. True cold-weather specialists, the mammoths' thick fur enabled them to thrive during the Ice Age, but as the world's climate warmed—and humans became ever more social and skillful group hunters—their numbers began to dwindle. The final mammoths are believed to have died out due to a combination of climate change and overhunting around 4,000 years ago.

◆ The thylacine, or Tasmanian tiger, was once common across much of Australasia before the arrival of Europeans—who destroyed its habitat and killed the foxlike "tigers" in enormous numbers, as they were considered a threat to farm animals and livestock—pushed the species to the brink of extinction. Although there have been isolated reports of thylacine in the remotest parts of the Tasmanian outback in the decades since, the last confirmed animal died in captivity at Hobart Zoo in 1936.

◆ Despite its name, the Irish elk—one of the largest deer species ever to have lived—once roamed widely across much of Europe and western Asia, before a combination of hunting and a warming climate caused the species to die out around 7,500 years ago. It is also likely that the sheer energy required by the animals to grow their enormous 12-foot-wide antlers each year might have simply proved too great as grazing land changed in the aftermath of the Ice Age.

◆ Astonishingly, the passenger pigeon was once the single most abundant bird species in the entirety of North America, with anything from three to five billion individual birds thought to have inhabited the continent. Despite these colossal numbers, the birds were widely hunted both for sport and food in the 19th century, and the entire population was wiped out. The last recorded bird, a lone female known as Martha, died in captivity at the Cincinnati Zoo in 1914.

TOP TEN: FASTEST ANIMALS

◆◆ **1** ◆◆

Peregrine falcon
(Maximum speed 242 mph)

◆◆ **2** ◆◆

Golden eagle
(150–200 mph)

◆◆ **3** ◆◆

Gyrfalcon
(130 mph)

◆◆ **4** ◆◆

White-throated
needletail swift
(105 mph)

◆◆ **5** ◆◆

Eurasian hobby
(100 mph)

◆◆ **6** ◆◆

Mexican free-tailed bat
(100 mph)

◆◆ **7** ◆◆

Frigatebird
(95 mph)

◆◆ **8** ◆◆

Rock dove
(92 mph)

◆◆ **9** ◆◆

Spur-winged goose
(88 mph)

◆◆ **10** ◆◆

Black marlin
(80 mph)

BOREDOM BUSTERS 6

What goes up but never comes down?

◆ ◆

The alphabet goes from A to Z, but I go from Z to A.
What am I?

◆ ◆

What copies what you say but never what you do?

◆ ◆

What gets less tired the more it runs?

◆ ◆

What has a head and a tail but no body?

(Find solutions on page 197.)

ART &
LITERATURE

WEIRDEST ARTWORKS

◆ Comedian is the title of a 2019 artwork by the Italian conceptual artist Maurizio Cattelan that consists of nothing more than a fresh banana attached to a wall using duct tape. The artwork is accompanied by precise instructions explaining how the banana and the tape should appear. Just three iterations of the work have been organized, with one—the second of the three—sold to cryptocurrency magnate Justin Sun for $6.2 million in 2024. Sun later ate the banana himself.

◆ French artist Marcel Duchamp was known for pushing the boundaries of the art world, but perhaps his most bizarre work was unveiled at an art competition in 1917. According to legend, Duchamp wanted to submit a work to the salon of the New York Society of Independent Artists, which accepted all submissions provided the artist paid the required application fee. Duchamp presented the society with an upturned urinal—signed "R. Mutt, 1917"—under the title Fountain. The artwork was unceremoniously rejected from the contest, and Duchamp, who was a member of the salon board, resigned in protest.

◆ Two years earlier, in 1915, Duchamp exhibited a piece known as Prelude to or In Advance of the Broken Arm—which consists of nothing more than an unused snow shovel, suspended on a wall. The artwork is currently on display at the Yale University Art Gallery in New Haven, Connecticut.

◆ Another surrealist artist known for pushing boundaries was Salvador Dalí, who in 1936 unveiled his Lobster Telephone—a work of art that, as its name suggests, consists of an old rotary-dial telephone, with a plaster lobster sitting atop the receiver. After the work became well known around the world, Dalí wrote that he was surprised he never received a "boiled telephone" whenever he ordered lobster in a restaurant.

◆ First exhibited as part of the Turner Prize display in 1999, one of the English artist Tracy Emin's most celebrated works is her "sculpture" My Bed—which comprises nothing more than her unmade bed, surrounded by a variety of objects and personal items, including a bedside table, crumpled papers, a toy cat, and a blue rug.

HOW J.R.R. TOLKIEN HELPED TO WRITE THE DICTIONARY

Although best known today as the author of both *The Hobbit* and *The Lord of the Rings*, besides his work as a writer of fiction, J.R.R. Tolkien was a skilled linguist and philologist who taught English language, literature, and Old English at the University of Oxford for over 30 years. It was in the years between his active service in World War I and taking up his position at Oxford in 1925, however, that Tolkien spent a year working on a project that was, at that time, known simply as a *New English Dictionary*.

The project would eventually become the hallowed *Oxford English Dictionary*, but at the time, its goal was merely to produce the most accurate record of the English language that had yet been undertaken. To do so, the team at Oxford required researchers and etymologists who could go through the many tens of thousands of paper quotations and citations that every word in their database had amassed, and chart the full history, origin, and definition of each one. Tolkien joined the dictionary's staff in 1919, and he was immediately given the task of researching and writing up all the entries between the words waggle and warlock.

The task was understandably immense, and it took Tolkien the next two years to chart the full histories and applications of all the words in his section—walnut, walrus, and wampum among them. And, although the *Oxford English Dictionary* has since had multiple revisions and continues to be updated and expanded year on year, many of Tolkien's original definitions remain in place to this day.

A LIMITED VOCABULARY: A HISTORY OF "CONSTRAINED" WRITING

◆ The 1939 novel *Gadsby* by the American writer Ernest Vincent Wright contains not a single letter E among its 50,000 words. As such, it is perhaps the most famous example of a writing technique known as a "lipogram," in which a particular letter or group of letters is deliberately avoided.

◆ While an acrostic poem or puzzle is a work of writing in which the first letter of each successive line spells out a hidden word or phrase, an abecedarius is a specific kind of work of acrostic writing in which each successive line or verse begins with a different letter of the alphabet in order, A to Z. Although several writers and poets have undertaken poems of this kind over the years, perhaps the most well-known example is Geoffrey Chaucer's poem "ABC," written some 700 years ago.

◆ A tautogram is an extraordinary style of writing in which all (or most) of the words in a given text begin with the same letter. The 1974 novel *Alphabetical Africa* by Walter Abish takes this technique to extremes, with the first chapter only containing A-words, the second containing A- and B-words, the third containing words beginning with A, B, and C, and so on. Halfway through the book, however, Abish reverses course and begins removing one letter in turn from chapter 26 onwards, until the final chapter contains solely A-words once again.

◆ "The quick brown fox jumps over the lazy dog" is a famous example of a pangram—a text that contains every single letter of the alphabet at least once. Since it became widely known in the early 1900s (when it was likely invented as a test or training exercise for typists), linguists and wordplay enthusiasts alike have attempted to write ever shorter pangrams, with the ultimate goal being a sentence that contains all 26 letters of the alphabet and none other. Incredibly, a handful of these so-called "perfect" pangrams have been engineered over the years, including "Mr. Jock, TV quiz PhD, bags few lynx."

◆ "Pilish" is a curiosity of constrained language in which the length of successive words in a sentence or passage of text follows the decimals of pi. The mnemonic "How I wish I could calculate pi" has been used for many years to remember the digits of pi to six decimal places (3.141592), but in 1996 the American mathematician Mike Keith took this technique to a new extreme, with all the words in his story Cadaeic Cadenza following pi's first 3,835 decimal places.

THE SHIPWRECK THAT INSPIRED SHAKESPEARE

I t is well known that many of Shakespeare's plays are based on true historical figures and events, and his plays included potted retellings of the lives of the likes of Richard III, Henry IV, and Henry V. Of all his plays to have been inspired by real-life events, however, perhaps the most surprising is his final play, *The Tempest*.

It was on June 2, 1609, that a ship called the *Sea Venture* departed Portsmouth, on the south coast of England, heading for Jamestown as part of a wider convoy of colonial vessels. Toward the end of July, however, the ships encountered a tropical storm in the mid-Atlantic, and while the others managed to sail around it, the *Sea Venture* was caught right in the storm's midst and became separated. Facing the loss of his ship, the *Sea Venture*'s captain took what he believed to be the best course of action and deliberately ran the ship aground on the rocks near the only nearby land, Bermuda.

Incredibly, the survivors of the *Sea Venture* remained stranded on Bermuda for the next nine months—during which time the other vessels continued on their way to America and reported the ship and all its passengers lost. Eventually, however, the survivors were able to use timber from the wreckage and trees from the island to construct two smaller ships, christened the *Deliverance* and the *Patience*. They eventually completed their journey, arriving in Jamestown in May 1610.

When news of their remarkable tale eventually reached England, it understandably caused a sensation—and reportedly inspired William Shakespeare to write one final play, *The Tempest*, about shipwreck survivors trapped on a magical island.

WORDS INVENTED BY WRITERS

Blatant
Edmund Spenser

Honeytrap
John le Carré

Boredom
Charles Dickens

Meme
Richard Dawkins

Chortle
Lewis Carroll

Muscleman
James Fennimore Cooper

Cyberspace
William Gibson

Pandemonium
John Milton

Doormat
(in the sense of a
weak-willed person)
Charles Dickens

Serendipity
Horace Walpole

Factoid
Norman Mailer

Tween
J.R.R. Tolkien

Freelance
Sir Walter Scott

Utopia
Thomas More

J.D. SALINGER AND THE D-DAY LANDING

S uch was the sheer scale of the effort and quantity of troops required, a surprising number of famous faces and names were involved in the D-Day landings of June 5, 1944, including the actor Henry Fonda, MLB star Yogi Berra, and future *Star Trek* star James Doohan. Also among the troops to have found themselves embroiled in action on the beaches of Normandy that day was the American author and writer J.D. Salinger—who, incredibly, had a draft of his novel *Catcher in the Rye* in his bag with him as he landed.

A sergeant in the 4th Infantry Division, J.D. Salinger (known as "Jerry" to his fellow soldiers) was initially meant to be in the first wave of troops on the morning of D-Day, but the plans were changed at the last minute, and he found himself in the second wave, due to land ten minutes later. Rough seas sent his ship a little off course, and he landed around a mile south of the intended destination, in a somewhat quieter and less exposed part of Utah Beach. And from there, he and his men headed inland.

On August 25, after some of the fiercest fighting of the entire war in the north of France, Salinger arrived in Paris—finding to his surprise that a fellow author, Ernest Hemingway, was in the city too. Reportedly, Salinger hopped in an army jeep and sped to the Ritz, where Hemingway was staying, and the pair talked over his latest story before Salinger and his men were recalled and marched back out of the city to continue the war effort. He went on to fight in the Battle of the Bulge, pushing hard into Nazi Germany, and was eventually involved in the liberation of Buchenwald concentration camp. On his return to America in 1945, Salinger published the first of two short stories he had been working on during his time in Europe, "I'm Crazy" and "Slight Rebellion at Madison." With both warmly received in the *New Yorker*, Salinger continued to hone the stories' chief character over the years that followed, before eventually introducing his readers to Holden Caulfield in his masterpiece *The Catcher in the Rye* in 1951.

HOW DICKENS' "A CHRISTMAS CAROL" CAME TO BE

C harles Dickens' "A Christmas Carol" is one of the most enduringly popular festive stories, and it has been adapted for television and film on dozens of occasions. The story behind the story itself, however, suggests its creation was far from festive for its author!

By the time he came to write "A Christmas Carol" in the early 1840s, Dickens was approaching the height of his success and had enjoyed a string of blockbuster novels with the likes of *Nicholas Nickleby*, *Oliver Twist*, and *The Old Curiosity Shop*. Despite strong sales, however, Dickens' relationship with his publishers was souring, and his latest novel, *Martin Chuzzlewit*, was proving so unpopular with readers that they were threatening to cut his pay. Money was now running low, and—against a backdrop of what he saw as increasingly unjust treatment for the poorest in society—Dickens resolved to write a short story that would both provide a cutting social commentary for the time and revive his fortunes.

Incredibly, Dickens pulled together "A Christmas Carol" in a flurry of creativity, writing 30,000 words in just six weeks. Still, his publishers were unsure, so Dickens bravely risked everything by paying for the publication himself; the risk paid off, and the book sold all 6,000 copies of its first print run by Christmas Eve. Within a year, it had gone to its 11th printing.

Despite this, however, the book did little to revive Dickens' financial situation. Ever the perfectionist, he spent far more than he had anticipated producing the finished product, even going so far as to turn down two early printings and bindings at considerable expense because he disliked the color. The individual copies he finally went with were so expensive to print, moreover, that even after a year of robust sales, he only cleared a profit of around £700, far less than he was hoping for. Nonetheless, "A Christmas Carol" caught the public's imagination perhaps like no other story before it, and Dickens' reputation and popularity with his readers skyrocketed. The story itself remains one of his best-known and most loved to this day.

TOP TEN: MOST EXPENSIVE PAINTINGS

◆◆ 1 ◆◆
Salvator Mundi
Leonardo Da Vinci
($450 million, 2017)

◆◆ 2 ◆◆
Interchange
Willem de Kooning
($300 million, 2015)

◆◆ 3 ◆◆
The Card Players
Paul Cézanne
(c. $250 million, 2011)

◆◆ 4 ◆◆
Nafea Faa Ipoipo (When Will
You Marry?)
Paul Gauguin
($210 million, 2014)

◆◆ 5 ◆◆
Number 17A
Jackson Pollock
(c. $200 million, 2015)

◆◆ 6 ◆◆
The Standard Bearer
Rembrandt
($198 million, 2022)

◆◆ 7 ◆◆
Shot Sage Blue Marilyn
Andy Warhol
($195 million, 2022)

◆◆ 8 ◆◆
No. 6 (Violet, Green and Red)
Mark Rothko
($186 million, 2014)

◆◆ 9 ◆◆
Wasserschlangen II
Gustav Klimt
($183.8, million 2013)

◆◆ 10 ◆◆
Pendant portraits of Maerten
Soolmans and Oopjen Coppit
Rembrandt
($180 million, 2016)

BOREDOM BUSTERS 7

You live in a huge single-story house, every single bit of which is made entirely of brick. So, what are the stairs made from?

◆◆

What can you break using only your voice?

◆◆

A man was outside in the pouring rain, without a hat, a coat, an umbrella, or anything that might have kept him dry—and yet not a single hair on his head got wet. How?

◆◆

Why is an iron cable like a cat?

◆◆

What gets harder to catch the faster you run?

(Find solutions on page 197.)

FAMOUS PEOPLE

WHEN A MET B: UNLIKELY MEETINGS OF NOTABLE PEOPLE

◆ Although he was born in Ireland, *Waiting for Godot* playwright Samuel Beckett lived for much of his life in a remote village on the outskirts of Paris. One of Beckett's neighbors in the village, a Bulgarian farmer named Boris Rousimoff, had a young son whom Beckett would give rides to school in his pickup truck: the boy in question would grow up to be André the Giant.

◆ In 1959, Soviet leader Nikita Khrushchev traveled to America and, while there, took a tour of the famous 20th Century Fox studios and attended a lunch with several of its most famous contracted stars—including Marilyn Monroe. According to reports, Monroe had memorized a line of fluent Russian, taught to her by fellow actress (and fluent Russian speaker) Natalie Wood. Turning to Mr. Khrushchev midway through lunch, Monroe stunned him by suddenly stating, "We, the workers of 20th Century Fox, rejoice that you have come to visit our studio and country."

◆ In 1842, Charles Dickens traveled to the United States, where a message reached him from a little-known writer who wanted to meet with him to discuss all things literary. Dickens gamely agreed, and the pair met in a hotel in Philadelphia, spending rather a long time discussing the ins and outs of copyright law and the desire of the American writer to begin publishing his work in England. The author in question was Edgar Allan Poe.

◆ While studying in Europe as a teenager, Orson Welles allegedly accompanied a German teacher on a hike around Austria, which (much to Welles' surprise) happened to finish at a Nazi rally near Innsbruck. After the event, Welles took a seat at a nearby table for food and refreshment—inadvertently sitting beside Adolf Hitler. "He made so little impression on me that I can't remember a second of it," Welles later recalled. "He had no personality whatsoever. He was invisible."

◆ In 1984, Steve Jobs was invited to attend the birthday party of the late John Lennon's nine-year-old son, Sean. As a gift, Jobs gave the boy an early Macintosh computer, entertaining many of the party's guests with the Paint program that allowed users to hand-draw images on screen. Suddenly, a voice from behind Jobs asked if he could give it a try: it was Andy Warhol.

THE FIRST PERSON TO WIN AN OSCAR AND A NOBEL PRIZE

T hey're two of the most venerated prizes in global culture, yet incredibly, only a scant handful of people have won both an Academy Award and a Nobel Prize. Not only that, however, but the first person ever to make this extraordinary double was one of the greatest playwrights in the history of the English language.

The story begins in the mid-1930s, when a young Hungarian film producer named Gabriel Pascal was setting his sights on a remarkable feat: adapting some of the great George Bernard Shaw's stage plays for the big screen. The only problem was that Shaw—who had been awarded the Nobel Prize for Literature just a few years earlier, in 1925—was notoriously cautious about having his works made into movies.

Pascal was nonetheless undaunted and managed to arrange a meeting with G.B. Shaw in which he gamely convinced him to let him at least try to adapt the classic society comedy *Pygmalion*. Shaw uncharacteristically granted Pascal the rights to the story, on condition that he personally retain some creative control over Pascal's film—including its screenplay.

As a result, Shaw adapted his own play for the cinema, with the result being 1938's British-made classic *Pygmalion* starring Leslie Howard and Wendy Hiller. For his adaptation of his own play, meanwhile, Shaw went on to be awarded the 1938 Oscar for Best Writing—adding it to his Nobel Prize.

The film was such a success, moreover, that Shaw granted Pascal further access to his works, and in the years that followed, the pair went on to adapt *Major Barbara*, *Caesar and Cleopatra*, and *Androcles and the Lion* for the big screen.

QUOTES & COMEBACKS

◆ The American writer Edna Ferber was notably fond of wearing men's suits, leading the playwright Noël Coward to comment on seeing her that she looked "almost like a man." Quick as a flash, Ferber replied, "So do you."

◆ Nancy Astor was the first female member of the British parliament—an achievement that brought her into close quarters with some of Britain's tartest and most opinionated men. "If I were married to you, I'd put poison in your coffee," Lady Astor once famously quipped to future prime minister Sir Winston Churchill. "Madam," Churchill replied, "if I were married to you, I would drink it."

◆ Another female politician who felt the cutting edge of Churchill's wit was the Labour Party's Bessie Braddock, who bumped into an inebriated Churchill at a party in the 1950s. "Winston!" Braddock reportedly exclaimed, "you are drunk!" To which Churchill replied, "You're right, Bessie. And you're ugly. But tomorrow morning, I'll be sober."

◆ Churchill was reportedly just as cutting with his friends as he was with his political rivals. His pen pal, George Bernard Shaw, once wrote Churchill that he had kept him two tickets for the opening night of his latest play. "Impossible to come to first night," Churchill wrote back. "Will come to the second night, if you have one."

◆ The American conservative writer and socialite Claire Booth Luce once reportedly bumped into Dorothy Parker and quipped, "Age before beauty!" The ever-quick-witted Parker replied, "Pearls before swine!"

HIDDEN TALENTS

◆ Queen Elizabeth II spoke fluent French and was a trained mechanic.

◆ Oscar-winner Geena Davis is a keen archer, and in 1999 she competed in the play-offs to represent the US at the Sydney Olympics.

◆ Former NFL footballer-turned-television-star Terry Crews studied classical flute for eight years in childhood.

◆ *House* actor Hugh Laurie is an acclaimed pianist and has recorded several albums of jazz and blues music.

◆ Justin Bieber is a fan of Rubik's cubes and can speed-solve them in under two minutes.

◆ Steve Carrell is a talented ice skater and hockey player, and in childhood he was a member of a youth team that won a national competition.

◆ Mark Ruffalo is a unicyclist.

◆ Late *Friends* actor Matthew Perry was a nationally ranked junior tennis player in his native Canada and was once ranked in the national Top 20.

QUIZ: MIDDLE NAMES

Listed on the left here are ten famous people—and jumbled together on the right are their middle names. Match the pairs together.

A Adele		**1** Bass
B Courteney Cox		**2** Blue
C Elton John		**3** Garry
D Hugh Grant		**4** Hercules
E James Corden		**5** Karuna
F Jennifer Lawrence		**6** Kimberley
G Kate Hudson		**7** Mungo
H Melanie Griffith		**8** Richards
I Tina Fey		**9** Shrader
J Uma Thurman		**10** Stamatina

THE WORLD'S FIRST MUSCLEMAN COMPETITION (AND ITS UNUSUAL JUDGE)

I n 1894, a German strongman named Eugene Sandow opened a fitness and strength clinic—an "institute of physical culture," as he called it—on St. James' Street in central London. And as luck would have it, one of Sandow's neighbors was none other than *Sherlock Holmes* creator Sir Arthur Conan Doyle.

As well as being an acclaimed author, Doyle was also a trained physician and ran a practice just a few streets away from Sandow's clinic. His work in anatomy and physiology led Doyle to take an interest in Sandow's methods, and the two men struck up an unlikely friendship, with Doyle becoming one of Sandow's earliest and keenest clients.

Over the years that followed, the pair became close friends and training partners, so that when Sandow decided to host the world's first bodybuilding competition in 1901, Doyle gamely agreed to be one of the judges. Using his connections across the city, Doyle managed to secure none other than the Royal Albert Hall as a venue for Sandow's contest, and on September 14, a sold-out hall packed with 15,000 spectators played host to the event. Twelve finalists competed for a golden statuette and a prize of 1,000 guineas, with a competitor known only as Mr. Murry taking first place.

The event was such a success that not only have bodybuilding contests remained popular ever since but a whole new vogue for strength and fitness emerged in Edwardian England.

TIME FOR A DUEL

◆ President Andrew Jackson was involved in several duels throughout his life, many of them in the gallant defense of his wife, Rachel. Such was the case in 1806, when Jackson challenged a Tennessee attorney named Charles Dickinson to a duel, claiming that Dickinson had insulted his wife (and, in the process, suggested Jackson had cheated on a horse racing bet). The pair met on May 30, and although Dickinson was an accomplished shot—he fired first and struck Jackson in the chest—Jackson's injury was not fatal, and he managed to return fire, killing Dickinson.

◆ Vice president Aaron Burr famously dueled his longtime rival Alexander Hamilton in Weehawken, New Jersey, in 1804. Hamilton was shot in the chest and died the following day; although victorious, the death ruined Burr's political career.

◆ French author Alexandre Dumas fought a duel on a bitterly cold January morning in 1825, after his opponent had made scurrilous comments about his shabby appearance over dinner a few nights previously. The son of one of Napoleon's generals, Dumas was an accomplished shot (and, luckily, an accomplished swordsman— the duo's guns misfired, and the duel was eventually fought with blades), and he easily defeated his opponent.

◆ *War and Peace* author Leo Tolstoy recounted that he "killed men in war and challenged men to duels in order to kill them" in his autobiographical *Confession* in 1882, but perhaps the most famous duel of his life never actually came to pass. Having fallen out with his friend and fellow writer Ivan Turgenev, the pair agreed to duel—but after a long-winded back-and-forth of letters and arrangements, the two men reconciled before a single shot was fired.

◆ Future president Abraham Lincoln famously dueled with the State Auditor of Illinois, James Shields, in 1842, after Lincoln wrote an anonymous critique of him in the local press. The duel was fought with swords, and the six-foot-four-inch Lincoln managed to inadvertently bring down the bough of a tree on Shields' head as he swung his blade. The pair was eventually talked out of further fighting by friends, and the duel was over before it had truly begun.

TOP TEN: MOST FOLLOWED CELEBRITIES

T he most followed account on Instagram is actually the official @instagram account, with almost 650 million followers. Excluding businesses, the most followed celebrities on the social media site are currently as follows:

◆◆ 1 ◆◆
Cristiano Ronaldo, @cristiano
(652 million followers)

◆◆ 2 ◆◆
Lionel Messi, @leomessi
(505 million)

◆◆ 3 ◆◆
Selena Gomez, @selenagomez
(421 million)

◆◆ 4 ◆◆
Dwayne Johnson, @therock
(394 million)

◆◆ 5 ◆◆
Kylie Jenner, @kyliejenner
(393 million)

◆◆ 6 ◆◆
Ariana Grande,
@arianagrande
(376 million)

◆◆ 7 ◆◆
Kim Kardashian,
@kimkardashian
(357 million)

◆◆ 8 ◆◆
Beyoncé, @beyonce
(312 million)

◆◆ 9 ◆◆
Khloé Kardashian,
@khloekardashian
(303 million)

◆◆ 10 ◆◆
Justin Bieber, @justinbieber
(294 million)

BOREDOM BUSTERS 8

What falls but never breaks?

◆ ◆

What man stands upright without bones, blood, or nerves?

◆ ◆

What runs through a door but never enters or leaves?

◆ ◆

How will next year start and end?

◆ ◆

What grows in the cold, dies in the heat, and has its roots at the top?

(Find solutions on page 197.)

SCIENCE

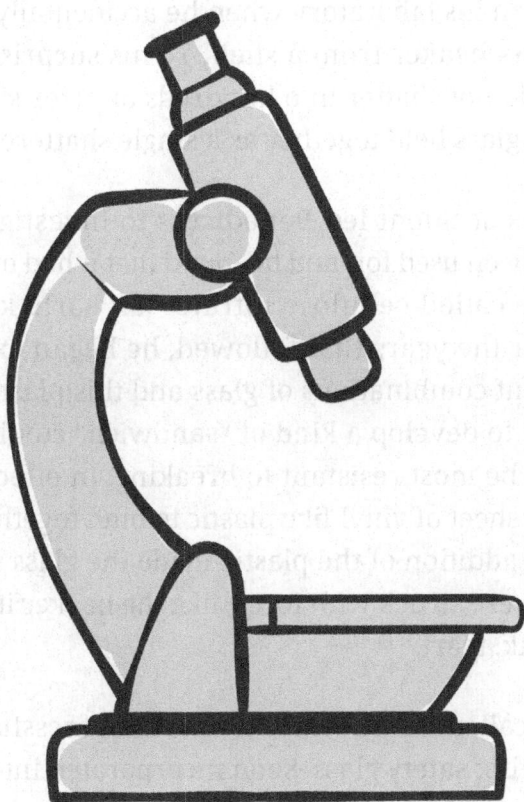

THE LABORATORY ERROR THAT MADE OUR CARS SAFER

I n 1903, a French chemist named Edouard Benedictus was working in his laboratory when he accidentally happened to knock a glass beaker from a shelf. To his surprise, the beaker broke but did not shatter into hundreds of razor-sharp shards—instead, the glass held together as a single shattered piece.

This curious accident led Benedictus to investigate what the beaker had been used for, and he found that it had once contained a substance called cellulose nitrate—an early kind of liquid plastic. Over the years that followed, he began experimenting with different combinations of glass and this plastic, eventually leading him to develop a kind of "sandwich" configuration that he found to be most resistant to breaking. In effect, Benedictus used a clear sheet of vinyl-like plastic to bind together two sheets of glass: the addition of the plastic made the glass shatter-proof, so that if it were struck with force, like the beaker it would break but not break apart.

Benedictus called his invention Triplex—successfully inventing the world's first safety glass. Soon incorporated into early motor vehicles, the glass improved road safety immeasurably and versions of this early concoction of cellulose and glass have been used in car windshields ever since.

BUNKUM! SCIENTIFIC THEORIES THAT HAVE BEEN DISPROVED

◆ One of the oldest theories in science was the so-called classical elements idea, which held that all matter comprises different combinations of a limited number of fundamental elements—most commonly, air, water, fire, and earth. The idea of fundamental elements remains as accurate as ever and has been the foundation of modern chemistry ever since the work of scientists like Antoine Lavoisier and Dmitri Mendeleev (the father of the periodic table). The idea that air, water, fire and earth are the building blocks of all things, however, has long since been debunked.

◆ The influential 18th-19th-century English chemist and physicist John Dalton is best known for his investigations of color blindness, which is still sometimes known as daltonism in his honor. He proved less successful, however, in his theories of the atom, having once believed that atoms were indivisible and unbreakable, and that all atoms of identical elements must have an identical mass— ideas that have since been disproved by nuclear physics and the discovery of isotopes.

◆ Because light travels in waves, it was once believed that space, rather than being a vacuum, was filled with an invisible medium called luminiferous ether—the only explanation scientists had for the ability of light waves to travel through what appeared to be complete emptiness. Experiments at the end of the 19th century, however, appeared to prove that not only did luminiferous ether not exist, but it was not needed at all.

◆ In the early 19th century, a scientist named Johann Friedrich Meckel posited that humans—as the most optimal life form—must undergo stages of development inside their mothers' wombs that correspond to the lesser life forms on earth. In essence, Meckel believed that human embryos undergo a "fish stage" at some point in their development, and the discovery of gill-like slits in the necks of early fetuses seemed for a long time to support his theory. Eventually, however, Darwin's theory of evolution proved that these developmental human "gills" were nothing more than a relic of our genetic past, as humans and fish share a common ancestor; the notion that humans develop, in utero, through life stages matching those of other life forms on earth was, ultimately, clearly misguided.

◆ Spontaneous generation was a theory that once held that life could arise, seemingly spontaneously, from non-living matter—a notion supported by the appearance of creatures like maggots in dead flesh. Supported by influential works by classical thinkers such as Aristotle, this theory was maintained from antiquity right through to the 18th century, when scientists in Europe first began to question it—and later, prove that creatures like maggots only appear if flies have access to decaying matter. The findings of this new era of scientific inquiry eventually led to the discovery of germs and cells, and later the entire field of microbiology.

◆ Prior to the 1700s, the burning of matter was said to be caused by the presence of a fire-like element in the matter known as phlogiston, which was said to be released via combustion. The eventual disproving of the classical elements theory not only proved that the makeup of matter is far more complex than once thought, but it also disproved the notion of the existence of phlogiston entirely.

WHAT HAPPENED TO EINSTEIN'S BRAIN

H e's one of the most famous scientists in history—and this part of his life story must surely be one of the most bizarre!

On April 17, 1955, Albert Einstein died in hospital in Princeton, New Jersey, having suffered an aortic aneurysm at the age of 76. The facts of his death were confirmed by an autopsy performed by Princeton pathologist Dr. Thomas Harvey (whose report also concluded that, despite a rumor to the contrary, he had not been suffering from syphilis at the time of his death). As Einstein's body was being prepared for his cremation, however, Dr. Harvey took the somewhat bizarre step of removing his brain for medical research—without the permission of his family.

Dr. Harvey then dissected and photographed Einstein's brain, taking images of thin slices of it using a microscope, before placing the 240 dissected samples and what remained of the rest of the brain in a jar. He then kept the preserved brain in a cider chest at his home, where it was found in his possession more than two decades later.

Dr. Harvey's behavior has long been called into question: although he was acting out of scientific curiosity and hoped that the world of neuroscience could benefit from his examinations, the fact that his dissections and photography were seemingly carried out without Einstein's family's permission has long been criticized. Dr. Harvey went on to lose his license on an unrelated issue, while Einstein's eldest son Hans, for what it was worth, later gave retrospective permission for his brain to be donated to science.

Ultimately, while the rest of Einstein's remains were quietly cremated and scattered at an undisclosed location, samples of his dissected brain remain in store at the Mütter Medical Museum in Philadelphia.

QUIZ: ELEMENTS THAT DON'T MATCH THEIR SYMBOLS

There are now 118 elements on the periodic table, from hydrogen to oganesson. And every element on the period table has its own symbol—from H to Og. Not every element quite matches its symbol as clearly as these two, however. Listed on the left here are the names of ten elements for which this is the case and jumbled together on the right are their non-quite-so-corresponding symbols. Can you match them up?

A Antimony		**1** Ag
B Gold		**2** Au
C Iron		**3** Fe
D Lead		**4** Hg
E Mercury		**5** K
F Potassium		**6** Na
G Silver		**7** Pb
H Sodium		**8** Sb
I Tin		**9** Sn
J Tungsten		**10** W

THE TRUMPETERS WHO PROVED THE DOPPLER EFFECT

I f you've ever stood on a sidewalk as a police car or ambulance drives by blaring its siren, then you have likely experienced the Doppler effect.

Also called "the Doppler shift," this curiosity of physics relates to how movement affects the production and reception of waves—and thereby explains why the pitch of a sound such as a siren or car horn appears to change as the object producing the sound moves toward and then away from the observer. When the object making the sound is moving toward the observer, each successive cycle of the sound wave it is producing is emitted from a point closer than the last. So, from the observer's perspective, at least, the time between each of the cycles of the sound wave is reduced, thereby increasing the frequency of the sound. As the object passes by and then begins moving away from the observer, conversely, each cycle of the wave is emitted further away than the last, producing the opposite effect.

The Doppler effect is named after Christian Johann Doppler, the Austrian physicist who first described it—based on his observations of train whistles—way back in 1842. A few years later, a fellow scientist named Christophe Ballot decided to test out Doppler's theory in a remarkably straightforward yet ingenious experiment.

None of the scientific instruments we can use to measure wave patterns existed in the 1840s, so Ballot had to be far more pragmatic. He arranged with a local train company to pull an open-topped trolley along a rail line, housed inside of which were a group of trumpeters. Stood on the platform of the station were another group of trumpeters, and both groups had tuned their instruments to the same note.

Beginning the experiment, Ballot had both groups of musicians play the same continuous note—but as the train passed by (roaring through the station at the unthinkable speed of 40mph!) the note being produced by the players in the trolley seemed to clash with those stood on the platform, first sounding a little too high and then, as the trolley passed by, a little too low.

Everyone in the station could hear the effect clearly, proving Doppler's theory once and for all.

HOW BLUETOOTH WORKS

I t's an ingenious technology that has revolutionized the modern world, allowing us to connect to our computers, laptops, mobile devices, and even our cars and other people's technology without any annoying wires. But how does a Bluetooth connection actually work?

Bluetooth devices simply emit weak radio waves along 79 different radio frequencies in a small band around 2.4 GHz. When you connect two Bluetooth devices together, one of these 79 frequencies is chosen at random, and the two devices look for one another on this random connection. Once linked, they remain connected with one another, hopping across the radio frequency multiple times a second, to maintain a solid and unbroken connection.

Because Bluetooth connectivity tends only to be needed over very small distances—say, from a headset to a desktop computer, or from a pair of earphones to a mobile telephone—the waves that they produce are very weak. This saves battery power, making Bluetooth technology remarkably efficient, thought it also limits them to a range of often only 20-30 feet. Once one or both of the connected devices steps outside of this range, the waves are not strong enough to maintain the radio link and the devices disconnect.

TOP TEN: LIGHTEST ELEMENTS

T he density of chemical elements is typically measured in g/ cm³ (grams per cubic centimeter). The heaviest naturally occurring element is osmium; a single square-centimeter block of solid osmium would weigh just over 22.5 g—more than twenty-five times that of an equivalently sized piece of wood. Many of the elements in the extended periodic table, however, likely have densities in excess of 25g/cm³, but given that so much of what is known about these elements' chemistry remains estimated and theoretical, these predicted values have been excluded from the lists below.

◆◆ **1** ◆◆
Hydrogen
(0.0000899)

◆◆ **2** ◆◆
Helium
(0.0001785)

◆◆ **3** ◆◆
Neon
(0.0008999)

◆◆ 4 ◆◆
Nitrogen
(0.0012506)

◆◆ 5 ◆◆
Oxygen
(0.001429)

◆◆ 6 ◆◆
Fluorine
(0.001696)

◆◆ 7 ◆◆
Argon
(0.001784)

◆◆ 8 ◆◆
Chlorine
(0.0032)

◆◆ 9 ◆◆
Krypton
(0.003749)

◆◆ 10 ◆◆
Xenon
(0.005894)

◆◆

TOP TEN: HEAVIEST ELEMENTS

1

Osmium
(22.59)

2

Iridium
(22.56)

3

Platinum
(21.45)

4

Rhenium
(21.02)

5

Neptunium
(20.45)

6

Plutonium
(19.85)

7

Gold
(19.3)

8

Tungsten
(19.25)

9

Uranium
(19.1)

10

Tantalum
(16.69)

BOREDOM BUSTERS 9

What might you find in an empty pocket?

◆◆

I have no beginning nor end, and nothing in the middle, but symbolize a new start. What am?

◆◆

What points the way, but never goes there itself?

◆◆

What boat is only useful when it has liquid on its inside?

◆◆

Poor people have it, rich people want it, and if you eat it you die. What is it?

(Find solutions on page 197.)

MYTHS & LEGENDS

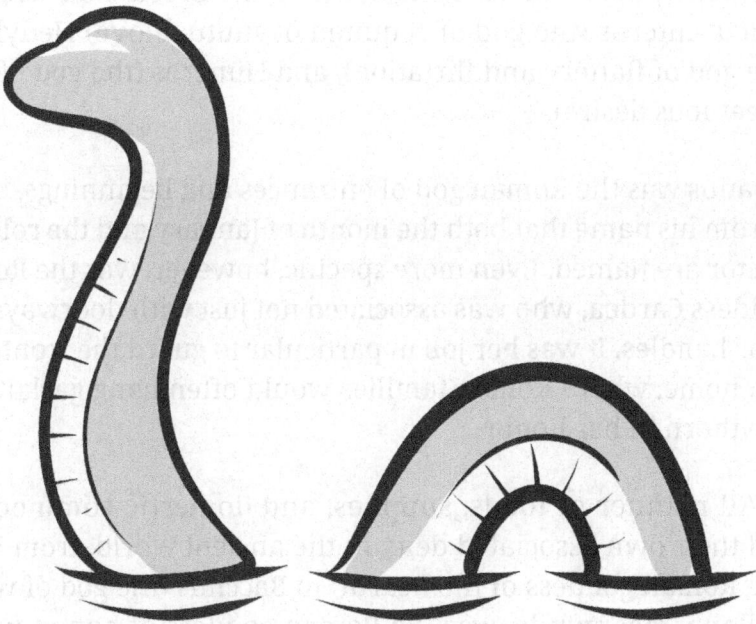

STRANGEST GODS

◆ The Romans were known for introducing city-wide sewage systems, and naturally, they had a goddess, Cloacina, whose role was to look after them.

◆ You've no doubt heard of the Greek god of love, Eros (and his cherub-like Roman equivalent, Cupid). But Eros was just one member of a group of romantic deities in the Greek pantheon called the Erotes, none of the rest of which were likewise adopted by the Romans. Alongside Eros, the Greeks had love gods called Anteros (the god of requited or mutual love) Hedylogos (the god of flattery and flirtation), and Himeros (the god of raw, impetuous desire).

◆ Janus was the Roman god of entrances and beginnings, and it is from his name that both the month of January and the role of a janitor are named. Even more specific, however, was the Roman goddess Cardea, who was associated not just with doorways, but door handles. It was her job in particular to guard the front door of a home, where Roman families would often hang garlands of hawthorn in her honor.

◆ All manner of foods, supplies, and domestic commodities had their own associated deity in the ancient world, from Vesta (the Roman goddess of the hearth) to Bacchus (the god of wine). Mellona, meanwhile, was the Roman goddess of honey, whose role also included the protection of bees.

◆ Taking his name from the Latin word for manure, Sterquilinus was a Roman god associated with lavatories, feces, and—perhaps less unpleasantly—the fertilization of agricultural land.

THE FIRST LOCH NESS MONSTER SIGHTING

I t was way back in 1933 that a local Scotsman named Hugh Gray took a now-famous grainy photograph of an unusually shaped creature apparently swimming just below the surface of Loch Ness in the Scottish Highlands. Different theories about precisely what Gray had photographed have been proposed over the years, from nothing more than a stretched-out canine, mid doggy paddle, to the bough of a tree, washed smooth and all but free of bark by the loch's waters. Others, of course, believe that Gray had taken the first-ever photograph of the now-legendary Loch Ness monster, and tales—and sightings—of Nessie have been reported almost continually ever since.

Gray might have taken the first photograph of the loch's supposed monster, but he was not the first person to record something mysterious in its waters. In fact, tales of a creature said to inhabit Loch Ness date all the way back to the sixth century!

According to local folklore, it was St. Columba—an Irish missionary and abbot who worked to spread Christianity in Scotland some 1,500 years ago—who first reliably recorded a sighting of the Loch Ness monster while staying nearby. Although different versions of Columba's story abound, at least one account claims that he was staying near the mouth of the River Ness in August of 565 CE, when he first heard tales of a creature living in the loch that had recently attacked some local people while they were swimming. Columba and one of his companion monks, Lugne, took it upon themselves to investigate, and as Lugne stepped into the waters, a giant monster emerged nearby and began swimming toward him, readying itself to attack.

Columba, however, was undaunted. Despite the apparent danger to his companion's life, he stepped forward, performed the sign of the cross, and demanded in the Lord's name that the creature retreat into the depths of the loch. One account even claims that the monster was within a spear's length of the monk before it seemingly heeded Columba's words and fled back beneath the water.

Some people have since claimed Columba's words are the reason why the Loch Ness monster remains so infrequently seen to this day, with the creature still heeding his demands almost a millennium-and-a-half later.

THE MAJOR SHIP LOST TO THE BERMUDA TRIANGLE

A nother mystery that has sparked stories and legends for centuries is that of the Bermuda Triangle. Ships have long since avoided this one million square-mile patch of the north-central Atlantic Ocean, which is typically said to correspond to a near-perfect triangle formed by the island of Bermuda, Miami in Florida, and the port of San Juan, on the north coast of Puerto Rico.

Since the mid-19th century, more than 50 ships and, more recently, dozens of seaplanes and aircraft, are said to have been mysteriously lost in this vast area of open ocean, with everything from swirling waterspouts to alien interference claimed to be at play. But of all the ships said to have vanished in the Bermuda triangle, perhaps one of the most famous—and mysterious—is the USS *Cyclops*.

The *Cyclops* was a collier ship that operated during World War I, ferrying supplies from the Caribbean and eastern seaboard to US vessels in European waters. Toward the end of the war, in March 1918, she was returning from a voyage to Brazil when she suddenly disappeared inside the Bermuda Triangle, seemingly with the loss of everyone and everything on board. No distress signal was sent, but when the ship's disappearance was finally realized, dozens of relief vessels went to try to locate her—fearing that she might have been struck by a German submarine—but no trace of the *Cyclops* could be found. To this day, the ship's complete disappearance remains a mystery, and no wreck has ever been discovered.

THE YETI'S FOOTPRINTS

T ales of giant ape-men living in wild areas are recorded all over the world, from Sasquatch in North America to the legendary Yowie of the Australian Outback. Each cryptid has countless tales of sightings attached to its name—but some of the most convincing evidence that these giant bipedal apes roam wild around the world comes from the Himalayan yeti.

Local mountain-climbing Sherpas in Nepal have long told tales of the giant solitary yeti said to inhabit the snowy peaks of the Himalayas, but ever since western mountaineers began to set their sights on summiting these enormous peaks in the early 1900s, such stories have only proliferated further. They reached new levels of fervor in 1951 when a mountaineer named Eric Shipton photographed a set of gigantic footprints he and his team had stumbled across in the snow of Mount Everest.

Shipton was part of a group of mountain climbers attempting to reach the top of Everest two years prior to Edmund Hilary's first successful summit in 1953. On spotting the footprints, around 15,000 feet above sea level, the team quickly reached for their cameras and took a series of snapshots; with no rulers or measures on hand to show the scale of the prints, they used ice picks and snow boots to prove that the feet that had left them were demonstrably larger than any human's.

Hoping to locate the source of the footprints, Shipton followed them for almost a mile along a glacier, where he made camp for the night and awaited the arrival of some other explorers from his team. When they arrived, they too examined the footprints and supported Shipton's claim that they surely must not be human.

On their return to England (having failed to summit Everest), news of Shipton's discovery quickly made headlines, but many people were quick to label the photos as a hoax. Others have suggested they were indeed human footprints, perhaps warped and distorted as the snow around them melted in the sunshine— while another theory claimed that they were merely left by local Nepalese hikers, as deformities of the feet are common injuries among them and abnormalities often go untreated in isolated communities.

To this day, however, the precise explanation for Shipton's photographs remains unclear.

QUIZ: MATCH THE GREEKS TO THE ROMANS

T he Greeks and Romans had numerous equivalent deities, as
the Romans adopted many of their gods and goddesses from
the pantheon of Ancient Greece. Match the Greek gods on the left
to their Roman equivalents on the right.

A Aphrodite   **1** Bacchus

B Artemis   **2** Diana

C Dionysus   **3** Jupiter

D Helios   **4** Luna

E Hephaestus   **5** Mercury

F Hermes   **6** Neptune

G Kronos   **7** Saturn

H Poseidon   **8** Sol

I Selene   **9** Venus

J Zeus   **10** Vulcan

(Find solutions on page 197.)

THE GREATEST FIGHTERS IN MYTH AND LEGEND

◆ Perhaps the most famous fighter and warrior of all myth is the ancient hero Hercules (or Heracles). A son of Zeus and Hera, Hercules is known for completing his Twelve Labors—impossible feats of strength and daring, including slaying the nine-headed Hydra and the fabled Nemean lion. In the end, however, Hercules was killed by his wife, Deianeira, who was tricked by the centaur Nessus into gifting him a tunic soaked in centaur blood. Nessus had told Deianeira that his blood would ensure Hercules would never love anyone but her, but it was in fact a powerful poison that (according to one version of the tale, at least) was so painful Hercules took his own life to end his suffering.

◆ Theseus was the hero of Athens who liberated his city from the tyrannical king Minos, who each year would send a band of locals into his labyrinth, on the island of Crete, where they were slain by the hideous Minotaur. Theseus managed to kill the creature and escape the labyrinth, with the help of his half-sister, Ariadne, who had fallen in love with him.

◆ The heroic exploits of Odysseus are recounted in both the *Iliad* and the *Odyssey*, the latter of which details his nightmarish ten-year return journey from the Trojan War. Facing shipwrecks, sea monsters, witches, demonic sirens, and a band of cyclops, Odysseus finally arrived home to his wife Penelope, slaying the suitors who had lined up to woo her in the event of his death.

◆ Perseus was the legendary son of Zeus who managed to slay the gorgon, Medusa. The gorgon's glance would turn a man to stone, but Perseus utilized a highly polished shield—a gift from the goddess Athena—so as to see Medusa without being affected by her glare.

◆ The hero Bellerophon is known for capturing and taming the legendary winged horse Pegasus, which he used to kill the monstrous chimera that had been attacking Lycia in Anatolia. His success in the battle, however, led Bellerophon to consider himself a god, and he rode on Pegasus' back to Mount Olympus—an act of hubris that angered Zeus, who knocked him from his horse and sent him tumbling to his death.

THE BIGFOOT CAUGHT ON VIDEO

It was back in 1967 that cowboys Bob Gimlin and Roger Patterson picked up a video camera near Bluff Creek, California, and recorded 59 seconds of some of the most remarkable cryptozoological footage in history: a giant, dark-furred ape-like creature walks on two legs through the wilderness and at one point turns back to the look directly at the camera.

The footage has been debated and analyzed ever since, with believers—including Gimlin himself, who reiterated his belief in a 2017 interview with CBC—contending that it is proof of the existence of Bigfoot. Others, however, claim that it is nothing more than an elaborate hoax, with the furry figure in the center of the footage merely a man in a fairly unconvincing gorilla suit.

What do the experts think? Well, as Gimlin later recounted, the footage was once shown to Hollywood special effects expert William Munns—known for his groundbreaking work on movies such as *Return of the Living Dead* and *Swamp Thing*—who commented that, "I was the best there was in special effects [at that time and] I couldn't have come up with anything close to a man in a suit that looked like that."

CRYPTIDS AROUND THE WORLD

◆ The rainforests of Java are said to be inhabited by gigantic condor-sized bats, called ahools, which are large enough to be capable of snatching people from open ground. Although naysayers will claim that ahool sightings are based on little more than misidentified birds of prey, the legends are nevertheless maintained in some Javanese communities.

◆ The Olgoï-Khorkhoï, or Mongolian death worm, is a giant worm-like creature said to inhabit the sands of the Gobi Desert. A single touch is said to be enough to kill a person—though anyone curious enough to even approach the worm is in danger, as various accounts claim it can spit venom or even shoot electricity.

◆ The jackalope is a legendary cross between a jackal and an antelope long said to inhabit the American Wild West. Although likely inspired by nothing more than taxidermists' jokes—with monstrous creatures pieced together, Frankenstein-style, from the skins and remains of different animals—tales of the jackalope have endured for decades, with the creature now considered the unofficial state cryptid of Wyoming!

◆ The wampus cat is a legendary human-headed (or human-faced) big cat, said to inhabit America's Appalachians. According to one tale, the creature was originally a woman who was cursed to transform into the monster having eavesdropped on a conversation.

◆◆◆

◆ The Ogopogo is a monstrous water creature said to inhabit Lake Okanagan in British Columbia, Canada. Sightings date back more than 200 years, with those who have apparently seen the creature describing it as a black-scaled serpent-like monster, some 40 feet long.

POTLUCK

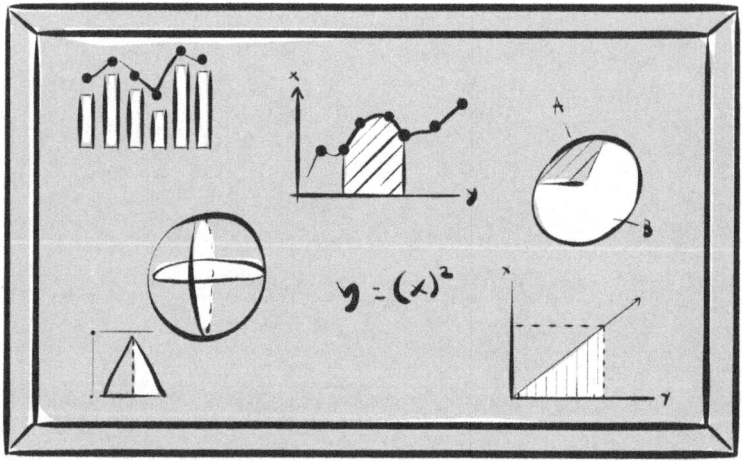

TAXICAB NUMBERS: THE MATHEMATICAL CURIOSITY SPARKED BY A LONDON CAB

In 1919, a renowned Cambridge University mathematician named G.H. Hardy was traveling to London to visit a former student and fellow mathematician, Srinivasa Ramanujan, who was in a hospital in Putney. Arriving in the city, Hardy hailed a cab to take him from the station to the hospital and found Ramanujan on one of the wards.

As the two began chatting, Hardy happened to note that he had traveled to the hospital in London taxicab number 1729 and joked that he hoped the cab's apparently arithmetically dull number wasn't a bad omen for Ramanujan's recovery. "No," he apparently countered, "it is a very interesting number—it is the smallest number expressible as the sum of two cubes in two different ways."

Ramanujan's astonishing quick thinking and arithmetic agility has since become legendary, and numbers sharing this quality have since become known as taxicab numbers. To date, only six such numbers have ever been discovered, of which 1,729—which is equal to both $1^3 + 12^3$ and $9^3 + 10^3$—is the second lowest. Technically speaking, the lowest of all taxicabs is 1 (as $1^3 + 1^3 = 1^3 + 1^3$)—but you'll have a long wait to get to the next one after 1,729, as it's 87,539,319!

WORDS BORROWED FROM OTHER LANGUAGES

◆ English has adopted very few words from Finnish, the majority of which are rather uncommon—including pulka (a kind of sled), motti (a kind of military or police tactic, in which an enemy is entirely encircled), and humppa (a jazzy style of Finnish music, based around a foxtrot). By far the best-known Finnish word we English speakers have adopted, however, is sauna.

◆ Meaning a remote rural area, boondocks can be traced back to a Tagalog Filipino word for a mountain.

◆ The word ketchup is said by some accounts to derive from the Malay name, kichap, for a kind of Chinese fish sauce. Malay is also the origin of running amok, which was originally the name of a kind of ferocious and murderous jungle madness.

◆ Long before it was an ice cream stand or a newspaper vendor's premises, a kiosk was a style of Turkish pavilion, known locally as a koshk or kioshk. From Turkey, the word was adopted into architectural parlance in French before finding its way into English in the 1600s.

◆ The word tattoo (in the sense of a permanent ink design on the skin) was introduced to English in the writings of the explorer Captain Cook, who picked it up from a local Polynesian language in the mid-1700s. Precisely what language the word is ultimately

◆◆

from is unclear, with various suggestions claiming the word is Tongan, Tahitian, or Samoan in origin.

◆ Although the word itself can be traced back to Arabic, English adopted the word safari from Swahili. It literally means "journey."

EPONYMOUS BODY PARTS

◆ The artery of Adamkiewicz is a major internal artery of the vertebrae, also known more technically as the major anterior segmental medullary artery. It is named after 19th-century Polish pathologist Albert Wojciech Adamkiewicz, who was known for his contributions to our understanding of the blood vessels around the spinal column.

◆ The pancreatic islets are a structure in the pancreas consisting of its major endocrine (i.e., hormone-producing) cells. They were discovered by a German pathologist named Paul Langerhans in 1869 and are ultimately also known as the islets of Langerhans.

◆ The canals of Schlemm are a series of tiny vessels in the eyeball that transport aqueous humor, the liquid found inside the eye. They are named after the 19th-century German anatomist Friedrich Schlemm, who discovered both them and the nearby nerve system of the cornea.

◆ Darwin's tubercle is a slight thickening of the outer curve of a person's ear, which is an evolutionary hangover only observable in around 10–40% of the population (depending on location). Given that it is a remnant of our evolutionary ancestors, the tubercle takes its name from Charles Darwin—although he himself referred to it as the Woolnerian tip, in honor of a British sculptor, Thomas Woolner, who once depicted it in one of his works.

◆ The tiny vibrating hair cells of the inner ear are contained in the so-called organ of Corti, which is named after the Italian anatomist, Alfonso Giacomo Gaspare Corti, who discovered it in 1851.

◆ The popping of your ears, meanwhile, is caused by the equalization of pressure inside vessels called the eustachian tubes—which take their name from the Italian scientist Bartolomeo Eustachi, aka Eustachius, who described them in 1552.

PRESIDENTIAL PETS

All but three US presidents—namely James K. Polk, Andrew Johnson, and Donald Trump —have had a pet during their time in the White House (although Johnson would reportedly feed the mice in his bedroom). Alongside cats and dogs, however, many other presidents throughout history kept some extraordinary animals in Washington, many of which were gifts from foreign dignitaries over the years.

Thomas Jefferson
Dick, a mockingbird

John Quincy Adams
an alligator (allegedly)

Martin Van Buren
two tiger cubs (later donated to a zoo)

William Henry Harrison
Whisker, a goat

James Buchanan
two Thai elephants**

Theodore Roosevelt
Josiah, a badger

William Taft
Mooly Wooly and Pauline, two cows

Calvin Coolidge
Rebecca, a raccoon, and Billy, a pygmy hippopotamus

Woodrow Wilson
a flock of sheep

*** Sadly, Buchanan's elephants, a gift from the King of Siam, arrived too late for his presidency; his successor, Abraham Lincoln, instead wrote to the king in 1862 saying, "I appreciate most highly Your Majesty's tender of good offices in forwarding to this Government a stock from which a supply of elephants might be raised on our own soil ... Our political jurisdiction, however, does not reach a latitude so low as to favor the multiplication of the elephant, and steam on land, as well as on water, has been our best and most efficient agent of transportation in internal commerce."*

THE FEYNMAN POINT

Although it is famously irrational, at the 762nd digit of the mathematical constant pi begins a sequence of six consecutive nines. Given that its digits appear so random elsewhere, this point in the digits of pi immediately appears unusual when written out—and indeed some mathematicians have calculated that the chances of a string of identical figures appearing so early on in the digits of a number like this is less than 0.1%.

With pi now extended into millions of decimal places, we now know that such identical strings are not too uncommon, and there are, in fact, seven consecutive nines at 1,722,776 decimal places in (and a further nine consecutive nines beginning at the 564,665,206th decimal place!). But this particular string is not only early in the number but has been given its own name: the Feynman point.

It is named in honor of the mathematician and physicist Richard Feynman, who once quipped that he wanted to memorize pi up to its 762nd place, and then say "Nine, nine, nine, nine, nine, nine, and so on!" implying that the rest of the figure continued in exactly the same way.

BIZARRE FLAGS

◆ The flag of the Isle of Man, in the British Isles, features a symbol of three interconnected armored legs, bent at the knee. The symbol, called a triskelion, is an ancient pre-Christian image that also appears on the flag of Sicily.

◆ The flag of Mozambique features an emblem consisting of a hoe and an AK-47 assault rifle.

◆ The flag of Nepal is the only national flag in the world that is not square or rectangular. Instead, it consists of two triangular pennants, one atop the other.

◆ The flag of Bermuda features the island's coat of arms, in the center of which is a shield depicting a shipwreck.

◆ In 1897, a British expedition to West Africa brought back to the UK a flag—often wrongly said to be the flag of the Benin Empire—depicting one man decapitating another with a sword. The precise history and origin of the flag, and which nation or tribe it was the emblem of, remain unclear.

NAMES FOR THINGS YOU DIDN'T KNOW HAVE NAMES

◆ The slight indentation in the upper lip is known as the philtrum. It takes its name from a Greek word for a love potion.

◆ A staircase that turns at 90°, rather than forming a landing, will have at its corner a series of slightly diamond- or rhombus-shaped stairs that are properly known as kite-winders.

◆ The long opening that can be seen through a series of arches or doorways that are perfectly lined up with one another is called an enfilade.

◆ The small brass or metal ring that holds an eraser at the end of a wooden pencil is called a ferrule.

◆ The glabella is the bare, usually hairless region of the forehead between the eyebrows.

◆ The protective cardboard sleeve slipped around a hot coffee cup is called a zarf. Originally, zarfs were ornamental cup-holders often made of silver or other precious metals, but the name has since become applied to any similar protective cover.

RANDOM MATH FACTS

◆ In a group of 23 people, there is a 50% chance that two of them will share a birthday.

◆ Two and five are the only prime numbers that end in two or five.

◆ The numbers on opposite sides of a die always add up to seven.

◆ The sum of all the numbers on a roulette wheel is 666.

◆ A googol is famously a number one followed by 100 zeroes. The term is not an official name, however, and in the proper arithmetic system, this number would be called ten duotrigintillion.

TOP TEN: LONGEST DICTIONARY WORDS

T he longest word in the entire English language is the full chemical name of a muscle-controlling protein, better known as titin, that, when written in full, has 189,819 letters. There isn't room for that word in print, alas (and most chemical terms like this are not included in the pages of a standard dictionary). According to Merriam-Webster, ultimately, the ten longest English dictionary words are:

♦♦ 1 ♦♦

Pneumonoultramicroscopicsilicovolcanoconiosis – a kind of lung condition caused by inhaling quartz dust
(45 letters)

♦♦ 2 ♦♦

Hippopotomonstrosesquippedaliophobia – a concocted word for, ironically, the fear of long words
(36 letters)

♦♦ 3 ♦♦

Supercalifragilisticexpialidocious – coined for *Mary Poppins*
(34 letters)

♦♦ 4 ♦♦

Pseudopseudohypoparathyroidism – a thyroid condition
(30 letters)

◆◆ 5 ◆◆

Floccinaucinihilipilification – the act of regarding
something as worthless
(29 letters)

◆◆ 6 ◆◆

Antidisestablishmentarianism – a 19th-century
political movement advocating the separation of church
and state in Britain
(28 letters)

◆◆ 7 ◆◆

Electroencephalographically – in a manner using a device for
recording brain waves
(27 letters)

◆◆ 8 ◆◆

Radioimmunoelectrophoresis – a term referring to a
technique for separating and identifying proteins
(26 letters)

◆◆ 9 ◆◆

Thyroparathyroidectomized – a surgical term describing a
patient who has had both their thyroid and parathyroid glands
removed
(25 letters)

◆◆ 10 ◆◆

Laryngotracheobronchitis –inflammation of the larynx,
trachea, and bronchi
(24 letters)

BOREDOM BUSTERS 10

What kind of cat are you most likely to find in a library?

◆◆

Why is an orange like a church tower?

◆◆

What is always in visible yet also in sight?

◆◆

What can you eat yourself but only drink when giving it to someone else?

◆◆

What kind of sweet-tasting apple never grows on apple trees?

(Find solutions on page 197.)

CONCLUSION

We started off by saying this was the book for the man who has everything. But if that were the case, then everything you've learned over these past few dozen pages would have been already known to you, right?

Perhaps we're getting ahead of ourselves, though, and perhaps there was the odd factoid here or there that you might have heard before. But given everything we've covered here—from the trumpeters who proved how sound waves work to the hippopotamus once housed at the White House—that's fairly unlikely.

I mean, had you really heard about the magical taxicab number, the radio waves that work your Bluetooth headset, and the Roman god of manure?

And who among us has knowledge encompassing the digits of pi, the shortest-performing Oscar-winners, and the finches' beaks that inspired one of the most groundbreaking theories in scientific history?

If all of that was already known to you before you started this book, then maybe you really did have everything!

SOLUTIONS

BOREDOM BUSTERS 1
A cold / A postage stamp / Ten / A goat / A decimal point

QUIZ: EPONYMOUS INVENTIONS
Named after their inventor
Mason jar (John L. Mason), Bunsen burner (Robert Bunsen), Stetson hat (John Batterson Stetson), Petri dish (Julius Petri), Ferris wheel (G.W.G. Ferris), Diesel engine (Rudolf Diesel), Jacuzzi (Jacuzzi brothers), Bakelite plastic (Leo Baekeland), Saxophone (Adolphe Sax), Biro pen (László Bíró), Zamboni (Frank J. Zamboni), Rubik's cube (Ernö Rubik).

Not named after their inventor
Trilby hat (named after the fictional hat wearer in the novel Trilby), Catherine wheel (named after St. Catherine, who was supposedly tortured on a wheel), Trombone (named for the Italian word for trumpet, tromba), Khaki fatigues (named for the Urdu word for dust).

BOREDOM BUSTERS 2
Legroom / One, two, and three / China / A seal (-se and al-) / Short

BOREDOM BUSTERS 3
A piano / Seven / All of them / A parachute / A clock

BOREDOM BUSTERS 4
A ton / Donald / Footsteps / Dust / Snow

SPORTING TERMINOLOGY QUIZ
A. 8, B. 5, C. 1, D. 9, E. 6, F. 3, G. 4, H. 7, I. 2, J. 10.

BOREDOM BUSTERS 5
A bottle / Alphabet / An egg / A sponge / A priest

BOREDOM BUSTERS 6
Your age / A zebra / An echo / A wheel / A coin

BOREDOM BUSTERS 7
There are no stairs / A silence / He was bald / It's a Fe line / Your breath

QUIZ: MIDDLE NAMES
A. 2, B. 1, C. 4, D. 7, E. 6, F. 9, G. 3, H. 8, I. 10, J. 5.

BOREDOM BUSTERS 8
Night / A snowman / A keyhole / With an N and an R / An icicle

QUIZ: ELEMENTS THAT DON'T MATCH THEIR SYMBOLS
A. 8, B. 2, C. 3, D. 7, E. 4, F. 5, G. 1, H. 6, I. 9, J. 10.

BOREDOM BUSTERS 9
A hole / A ring / A signpost / A gravy boat / Nothing

QUIZ: MATCH THE GREEKS TO THE ROMANS
A. 9, B. 2, C. 1, D. 8, E. 10, F. 5, G. 7, H. 6, I. 4, J. 3.

BOREDOM BUSTERS 10
A catalog / They both produce peels / The letter I / Toast / A pineapple

Made in United States
North Haven, CT
18 December 2025

85070777R00114